INTRODUCTION TO THE PRACTICE OF
AFRICAN AMERICAN PREACHING

Also by Frank A. Thomas

America 2.0: A Christian Way Out of the Great Recession
Preaching with Sacred Fire: An Anthology of African American Preaching from 1750–Present
Preaching as Celebration Digital Lecture Series and Workbook
They Like to Never Quit Praisin' God: The Role of Celebration in Preaching
The Choice: Living Your Passion Inside Out
The Lord's Prayer in Times Like These
Spiritual Maturity: Preserving Congregational Health and Balance
What's Love Got to Do with It?: Love, Power, Sex, and God
What's Love Go to Do with It?:
Love, Power, Sex, and God Companion Workbook

Visit Dr. Frank A. Thomas at
www.drfrankathomas.com
www.preachingascelebration.com

www.facebook.com/thepreacherscoach

follow Dr. Frank A. Thomas on Twitter
@drfrankathomas

Introduction to the Practice of
African American Preaching

Frank A. Thomas

Abingdon Press
Nashville

INTRODUCTION TO THE PRACTICE OF AFRICAN AMERICAN PREACHING

Copyright © 2016 by Abingdon Press

All rights reserved.
No part of this work may be reproduced or transmitted in any form or by any means, electronic or mechanical, including photocopying and recording, or by any information storage or retrieval system, except as may be expressly permitted by the 1976 Copyright Act or in writing from the publisher. Requests for permission can be addressed to Permissions, The United Methodist Publishing House, 2222 Rosa L. Parks Blvd., PO Box 280988, Nashville, TN 37228, or e-mailed to permissions@umpublishing.org.

Library of Congress Cataloging-in-Publication Data has been requested.

ISBN 978-1-5018-1894-3

Scripture quotations unless noted otherwise are from the Common English Bible. Copyright © 2011 by the Common English Bible. All rights reserved. Used by permission. www.CommonEnglishBible.com.

Scripture quotations marked (NRSV) are taken from the New Revised Standard Version of the Bible, copyright 1989, Division of Christian Education of the National Council of the Churches of Christ in the United States of America. Used by permission. All rights reserved.

The lecture "Seven Decades of African American Preaching" by Jeremiah A. Wright, Jr., presented March 4, 2015, at Christian Theological Seminary, is used by permission.

The sermon "His Own Clothes," by Gardner C. Taylor, is used by permission.

Chapter five, "The Truth Is Always Relevant," was originally published in *Homiletic* 41, no. 1 (2016) and is used with permission.

16 17 18 19 20 21 22 23 24 25—10 9 8 7 6 5 4 3 2 1
MANUFACTURED IN THE UNITED STATES OF AMERICA

*To the memory of William Scott Jr. and Jannie Lee Scott
for giving birth to Joyce Scott,
now Joyce Scott Thomas,
whom I love deeply
and will for all the days of my life.
I am eternally grateful.*

CONTENTS

Acknowledgments	ix
Introduction	1
Chapter One: The Bus Tour of the Study of African American Preaching	11
Folk Preaching and Educated Preaching	11
The Paucity of Academic Study of African American Preaching	16
The Study of African American Preaching before Martin Luther King Jr.	20
The Study of African American Preaching after Martin Luther King Jr.	29
African American Women and Womanists	36
Taxonomy of the Study of African American Preaching	46
Chapter Two: Negro Expression, Signifying, and the Rhetoric of African American Preaching	55
The Historical Relationship between Homiletics and Rhetoric	56
Zora Neale Hurston and the Oral Tradition of Black Preaching	69
Signifying and African American Preaching	74
Chapter Three: "It's Alright Now": A Rhetorical Analysis of Gardner C. Taylor's Sermon "His Own Clothes"	85
Characteristics of African American Preaching	86
Black Preaching: Henry H. Mitchell and Cleophus J. LaRue	88

– VII –

CONTENTS

Black Preaching and Rhetorical Criticism	91
Close Reading of "His Own Clothes"	97

Chapter Four: "Keepin' It Real": The Validity of the Existentially Authentic Performance — 111

Jay-Z and Criteria for the Real	113
The Logic of the Lyrics	115
The Emotional Truth That Supports the Lyrics	121
The Human Motivation the MC Fills In	125
Getting Even the Smallest Detail Right	129

Chapter Five: The Truth Is Always Relevant: Race and Economics in Contemporary African American Preaching — 135

The Truth Is Always Relevant	136
The Civil Rights Movement and the New Movement	138
The Bigger Subjects for Millennials and Gen-Xers	140
Tension Points: The New Movement and the Church	144
The Church and the New Movement	148
Taking the Long View	157

Afterword: "Seven Decades of African American Preaching" by Jeremiah A. Wright Jr. — 161

Selected Bibliography of African American Preaching — 179

Appendix A: "His Own Clothes" by Gardner Calvin Taylor — 185

ACKNOWLEDGMENTS

It is my hope and desire that this book would be a conversation, a "fierce conversation."[1] The term *fierce conversation* is borrowed from author Susan Scott, who defines the term *fierce* with synonyms such as robust, intense, strong, passionate, eager, and unbridled. In summary, she states that "a fierce conversation is one in which we come out from behind ourselves into the conversation and make it real," that is, we say something that is honestly and profoundly true for us.[2] For many, in popular vernacular, fierce means vehement, verging on being in attack mode, but it also can mean to be fervent and ardent about discovering the truth such that one is willing to put one's cards on the table or to become authentic about one's thoughts, feelings, and intentions, or even one's agenda. Scott remarks that while many are afraid of "real," it is the unreal conversation that should scare us to death. Therefore, let me put my cards on the table up front by stating several thoughts that are honestly and profoundly true for me.

First, my overall agenda and vision is to establish African American preaching as an academic discipline in its own right, and therefore, a full and equal partner with Euro-American, Latino/Latina, Korean, and other

---

1. The use of the term *conversation* in preaching is complicated by the fact of the "conversational school" of preaching, which is attempting to infuse the term *conversation* in the field of preaching with a technical meaning. The main proponents of this school are Lucy Atkinson Rose, John S. McClure, Joseph M. Webb, Ronald J. Allen, and O. Wesley Allen, Jr. My goal is conversation with those concerned with the craft of preaching—pastors, ministers, homiletic professors, seminary students, and interested laypeople. I believe the future of preaching is contained in the dialogue and conversations about preaching among many varied constituencies and perspectives, which explains again why I am using the term *fierce*.

2. Susan Scott, *Fierce Conversations: Achieving Success at Work & Life, One Conversation at a Time* (New York: Berkeley Books, 2002).

ACKNOWLEDGMENTS

preaching methodologies. The overall goal of this equality would be to ignite a preaching renaissance in America that would lead to a revival of American Christianity in the twenty-first century.

Second, because African American preaching is underresearched, and therefore underpublished, it is my hope that as an academic discipline there would be more titles in African American preaching and even a general series with an abundance of titles exclusively dedicated to publishing research and insights from the African American male and female preaching tradition.

Third, I was impressed when television producer and writer Shonda Rhimes delivered the 2014 commencement address at Dartmouth. She shared that, as a successful woman who is single and a mother of three, she is asked often, "How do you do it all?" She told the audience that while she had heard suggestions such as get help from other people, become more organized, and even try harder, she had learned that in the difficult task of juggling work and family it is not possible to have it all. Her conversation is fierce because she tells them that she will be 100 percent honest. She comes from behind herself and says what is honestly and profoundly true for her:

> If I am killing it on a *Scandal* script for work, I am probably missing bath and story time at home. . . . If I am succeeding at one, I am inevitably failing at the other. That is the tradeoff. That is the Faustian bargain one makes with the devil that comes with being a powerful working woman who is also a powerful mother. You never feel a hundred percent OK; you never get your sea legs; you are always a little nauseous. Something is always lost.[3]

This particular section of the speech touched me deeply because she was articulating my inner truth that I could not name. And while I will laud my passion and excitement in writing this book in the upcoming introduction, especially as a father and husband, I never feel 100 percent okay. I never get my sea legs. Endless hours of researching, reading, reflection, writing, and speaking takes me away from family time, movies, long

---

3. Shonda Rhimes, Dartmouth Commencement Address, June 8, 2014, www.dartmouth.edu/~commence/news/speeches/2014/rhimes-address.html.

walks, games, and just hanging out. Something is always lost. I am always a little nauseous and frenetic, because sometimes I am overwhelmed by it all. My editor, Connie Stella, sent me this line in an e-mail after I sent her an initial draft of this book: "Praying for stamina and energy as you get near the finish line." How did she know that I could see the finish line but was about to faint? How did she know that I needed a word of encouragement in the struggle of writing a book amidst a busy life?

I would like to thank my family, friends, and colleagues for their patience with my passion and preoccupation with African American preaching and all that comes with it. Special thanks to my wife, Joyce, daughter Rachel and her new husband Milton, and son, Tony. Thanks for understanding when the flight is late. Thank you for allowing me to read and write and sometimes be preoccupied with it. Thanks for riding with me to the library to pick up that one special book I need. Thank you for allowing me to share my gifts. Thanks to my parents, my sister and brother, who never fail to understand and ask when I pick up the phone, "Where in the world are you, now?" Thanks to Ronald J. Allen, President Matthew Myer Boulton, Bill Kincaid, Leah Gunning Francis, Rob Saler, Amelia Walker, Verity Jones, and the entire faculty and staff of the Christian Theological Seminary. Endless thanks are due to my preaching students, my pastor and homiletician friends. Thank you to these and many more for the support and encouragement that I had something vital and important to say.

Shonda Rimes concluded her graduation remarks by suggesting that she wanted her daughter to know her as a woman who works, a woman who runs Shondaland. She believes that she is a better mother because she gets to spend her days happy and fulfilled. She would not want her daughters to see a woman who was not whole. It is interesting that she never feels 100 percent okay, she admits that something is lost, and yet she is whole. I understand it because that is how I feel.

At the end of it all, I want my family, colleagues, and friends to see me as a person who cares deeply about relationships with them and African American preaching, and I am a better person for working on my passion. I get to run a center for African American preaching, develop the first ever PhD program in African American Preaching and Sacred Rhetoric. I get to think preaching, write preaching, do preaching, lecture on preaching, and talk about preaching. I get to think, write, reflect, dialogue, travel, experience, and expand my horizons, all with the goal to make the world a better place by proclaiming the genius of the African American preaching tradition. I still do not have my sea legs and I am happy, fulfilled, and whole. I am immensely thankful for all of the good things life has offered me.

Finally, I want to express my thanks to God Almighty. In her song "Golden," Jill Scott shares a strange and unique truth and prayer: she hopes God is proud of her.[4] She is talking about exercising her God-given freedom to use her gifts and talents to represent God's glory. She is living her life like it is "golden." Toward the end of the song she says that she is living her life like it is "important, like it matters, like it is special, like it is blessed." I agree with her. I am living my life like it is golden. Representing God's glory. God, I hope you are proud of me.

---

4. Jill Scott, "Golden," www.azlyrics.com/lyrics/jillscott/golden.html.

INTRODUCTION

From black pulpits and the mouths of impassioned black preachers, some of the most stirring and inspirational words of hope have come to this nation and the world down through the centuries and years. Much of this genius of the African American preaching tradition has been oral, and as such, has traveled for years in the oral tradition. While the oral tradition has tremendous strengths, one drawback has been that some of the best of African American preaching has gone to the grave because much of that genius was not captured or archived in written form. Or, if it was written down, it was not accessible to the wider community because it was and is located in church basements; in personal, denominational, and convention archives, newspapers, pamphlets, and the like; or in the hands of family members not sure how to get the genius out to the public. It is here that a critical need for scholars to research, explicate, capture, archive, and publish their findings on the African American preaching tradition locates itself.

Research and publication of the African American preaching tradition helps the tradition become an equal partner in homiletical discussions both in the American context and the global homiletical community, especially the Global South. The African American preaching tradition as an equal partner with Euro-American, Latino/Latina, Korean, and other preaching methodologies has the potential to ignite a preaching renaissance in America that could lead to a revival of American Christianity in the twenty-first century. There are many who laud the demise of Christianity in the Western world, and look for Christian growth exclusively in the Global South. I believe the contributions of African American preaching can impact significantly both a discussion with preaching in the Global

South and the pessimism and despair concerning Christian witness in the future of Western Christianity. I believe there is a deep need in the world for the genius of the African American preaching tradition to help revive Christianity in America in the twenty-first century and help shape important discussions of preaching around the globe.

I want the reader to know that the research, publication, and practice of African American preaching gives me deep gladness and great joy. So much so, that I have decided that, in my remaining years, it is my life's work to teach, preach, mentor, and share the genius of the African American preaching tradition with the world.[1] It is a passion that has deep roots in my life. Years ago, I was a young adult, who sat in the pew at the funeral services of a close friend in the neighborhood. He had been shot and killed as a part-time employee in a botched shoe store robbery. It devastated his family, the neighborhood, young adults, and especially me, because we were great friends. Everyone was grieving deeply, trying to make sense of the loss and sadness that was as thick as gray fog hanging over our lives and neighborhood. There is something especially poignant about the grieving of youth and young adults. I believe that these age groups often have the feeling of invincibility, and when death pierces that armor, it is especially wrenching and painful.

In the midst of the fog of death, the African American pastor of Emmanuel Baptist Church on the south side of Chicago, Reverend L. K. Curry, rose and preached the eulogy. When he finished, something had changed drastically in my soul. The preacher and the preached word had changed my outlook and perspective on the death. Amazingly, and to my surprise, I felt better. Though the travails of the grief process still lay ahead, I felt a sense of hope. I wondered what he did and how he did it. It was for sure the gospel message that I had heard most of my life, as I was a member of a church and educated in Christian schools, but it was drastically different. He made it relevant, fresh, alive, and real. I do not remember the text or the sermon itself, but I have never forgotten, as I

---

1. See my clarion call to the next generation entitled "A Call to the Ministry of the Scribe: Chronicling the African American Preaching Tradition," in Frank A. Thomas, *They Like to Never Quit Praisin' God: The Role of Celebration in Preaching* (Cleveland, OH: United Church Press, 2013), xiii–xvii.

heard a preacher say, "how it made me feel." Looking back these many years later, I realize that was the moment I fell in love with the power, beauty, healing, and depth of black preaching. Of course, I did not know it then, but that preaching moment was one of the factors of influence in my decision to accept my call to ministry, and for my own preaching of the gospel of Jesus Christ as a pastor, especially at such occasions of grief and loss. Subsequently, after finishing seminary, I served as the senior pastor of two outstanding congregations, for a total of thirty-one years.

As part of serving as a pastor, I estimated that I preached, on average, one hundred sermons per year for thirty-one years, for a total of at least three thousand one hundred sermons. While I have extensive practical experience in most aspects of congregational life, it was the preaching that gave me the most joy and life. It was with great love and thanksgiving that I preached those many sermons to meet the needs of the congregations and communities I was called to serve. I am grateful to both churches because it was a privilege to serve as their pastor, and as their pastor, being allowed to preach each Sunday and Wednesday night, plus funerals, celebrations, and other important occasions in the church and the broader community. In all of my preaching, I hoped and fervently prayed that the preached word of God would change perspectives and outlooks as the preaching ministry of L. K. Curry had changed mine.

Because I loved preaching so deeply, wanted to improve as a preacher, and tried to always offer my very best in excellence and effectiveness, I studied with the "father of black preaching," Henry H. Mitchell, and completed my doctor of ministry degree under his mentorship. My doctoral thesis, *They Like to Never Quit Praisin' God: The Role of Celebration in Preaching*, subsequently became a book that many regard as a continuation of Mitchell's work. In truth, I did not enroll with Henry H. Mitchell and Edward L. Wheeler at United Theological Seminary in Dayton, Ohio, to get a degree or write a book. I went because I loved preaching and wanted to work at it to get better at my craft by studying with a preaching scholar whose work I respected deeply. After all these years, I still believe that one of the greatest and most helpful books in the homiletical canon is Mitchell's *The Recovery of Preaching*.[2]

As a result of my improving skills in preaching, and my conversation with pastors about significant books in preaching that would help improve their preaching, I began to be asked to lead seminars in preaching in local churches. I was invited to teach associate ministers and many novice preachers around Chicago, which evolved into my first preaching classes. In 1989, teaching preaching in the community led McCormick Theological Seminary (Chicago) to invite me to teach as an adjunct professor in their master of divinity program. For over twenty-seven years now, I have taught preaching to master of divinity students at McCormick. This teaching experience and the publication of *They Like to Never Quit Praisin' God: The Role of Celebration in Preaching* led to further teaching as an adjunct professor at Luther Theological Seminary (Minneapolis), Chicago Theological Seminary (Chicago), North Park Theological Seminary (Chicago), United Theological Seminary (Dayton), and Garrett Evangelical Seminary (Evanston). Since 1995, I have served as adjunct professor in the Association of Chicago Theological Schools (A.C.T.S) doctor of ministry in preaching program. I am in my twenty-first year teaching in that program. I taught all these classes because I love the study and practice of African American preaching. The more I taught, the more I learned, and I noticed that my own preaching steadily improved. I have discovered the truth of the old adage that the person who learns the most in any class is the teacher of that class. From the students and their interaction with the materials, I gained more and more insights into the science, art, and craft of preaching.

Based upon my love of preaching, I decided to go back to school for more formal study of African American preaching and graduated from the University of Memphis with a doctor of philosophy degree in communication (rhetoric). My dissertation title was "I'm Happy Tonight: Martin Luther King Jr.'s Discourse of Prophetic Reconciliation." Under the tutelage of the rhetorical scholar and luminary, Michael Charles Leff, I explored the preaching and rhetoric of Martin Luther King Jr. in the

---

2. Henry H. Mitchell, *The Recovery of Preaching* (New York: HarperCollins, 1977).

last year of his life, from his noted speech at the Riverside Church in New York City, on April 4, 1967, entitled "Beyond Vietnam," to his last sermon, "I've Been to the Mountaintop," at Mason Temple in Memphis, Tennessee, April 4, 1968. It gave me great joy to study with this kind of intensity the preaching of Martin Luther King Jr. I learned a tremendous amount about the African American preaching tradition from a different and distinct angle than the traditional angles of theological inquiry. I studied African American preaching from the perspective of rhetoric and rhetorical processes. My study with Michael Charles Leff and the communications department at the University of Memphis gives this book, and my approach to preaching, a distinctive purpose: to develop African American homiletical theory that proposes black preaching is inherently theological and rhetorical.

At the conclusion of the doctoral degree, by the avenue of God's grace and mercy, and though it took nine years of my life, Martha Simmons and I completed *Preaching with Sacred Fire: An Anthology of African American Preaching, 1750 to the Present*. I have never taken on a more grueling and yet more rewarding project. This groundbreaking anthology includes 103 African American sermons since 1750, inclusive of male and female preachers, mostly Christian, and several non-Christian preachers. This book has proven to be an invaluable resource in the study and teaching of African American preaching. It is a systematic attempt to archive the genius of the African American preaching tradition. It was the work of joyful vocation, and I look forward to the next anthology to improve and go beyond *Preaching with Sacred Fire*. It is not my task to author, or co-author, the next anthology. My hope is that it will be done by a student or students whom I am privileged to mentor.

Presently, I am the Nettie Sweeney and Hugh Th. Miller professor of homiletics at Christian Theological Seminary (Indianapolis) and also the director of the Academy of Preaching and Celebration. The Academy of Preaching and Celebration is the only academy exclusively dedicated to African American preaching. I am also privileged to direct the very first PhD program in African American Preaching and Sacred Rhetoric. At this point, we hope in six years or so to release eight to ten doctoral scholars to the world in African American preaching. I am blessed with the privilege to live my vocation and passion, to teach preachers to preach the gospel of Jesus Christ, and to shape and influence preachers to rise to the height, depth, and beauty of the preaching ministry of L. K. Curry. This book is part of my vocation and my life's work, and I write it with great joy.

With all of that said, the reader is probably asking, so what is *Introduction to the Practice of African American Preaching* really all about? This book is a primer for African Americans and others who want to understand the African American preaching tradition by becoming aware of the historical development of the study of African American preaching, the distinctiveness of expression of African American preaching, models and modes of excellence in African American preaching, future trends in black preaching, and all set within the context of acknowledgment of the inherent relationship of theological and rhetorical processes. The unique contribution of this book is the emphasis and clarification of rhetorical processes in African American preaching. Because the reader is probably most familiar with theological processes, let me quickly outline what I mean by rhetoric and rhetorical processes.

As I will further outline in chapter 2, "Negro Expression, Signifying, and the Rhetoric of African American Preaching," African American preaching is an inherently theological and rhetorical act. Concurring with homiletical scholars Lucy Lind Hogan and Robert Reid, the rhetorical scholar Karlyn Kohrs Campbell defines rhetoric as "the study of all the processes by which people influence each other through symbols, regardless of the intent or the source"; therefore, rhetoric is concerned with "social truths, addressed to others, justified by reasons that reflect particular cultural values."[3] Kohrs Campbell's view is that human beings are always communicating because little that we say or do does not have persuasive effect or influence, and is therefore rhetorical. Kohrs Campbell distinguishes rhetoric from the rhetorical act, suggesting that the rhetorical act is "an intentional, created, polished attempt to overcome the obstacles in a given situation with a specific audience on a given issue to achieve

---

3. Lucy Lind Hogan and Robert Reid, *Connecting with the Congregation: Rhetoric and the Art of Preaching* (Nashville: Abingdon Press, 1999), 9.

INTRODUCTION

a particular end."[4] Unequivocally, in my view, a sermon is a rhetorical act. Historically, in the African American tradition, the nomenclature of "sacred rhetoric" was used to express the particularly rhetorical nature of the theological sermon. Donna E. Allen defines sacred rhetoric as "the actions humans perform when they use verbal and non-verbal symbols for the purpose of communication with one another about God."[5] I will clarify my argument in great detail in succeeding chapters, but I wanted the reader to recognize, as early as possible, one of the cardinal claims of this book: black preaching is inherently rhetorical and theological.

Before outlining the book, let me say one more word about the preparation and the development of the three critical questions that I respond to that shapes the heart of the book. In order to assist my thinking and research for the writing of *Introduction to the Practice of African American Preaching*, across two years, I convened separately two important and distinct groups within the broad scope of the African American preaching tradition: twenty-two homileticians, who teach and publish scholarship on African American preaching (April 2014), and twenty-five African American pastors, who practice preaching to congregations on a weekly basis (April 2015). My assumption was that much could be learned in discussions with professors of preaching and practicing preaching pastors in congregations. In April 2016, I held a joint meeting of these two groups so as to continue critical discussions of African American preaching.

In the 2014 and 2015 meetings, I followed a similar format and asked each group to respond to three critical questions: (1) What is black preaching? (2) What is excellence in black preaching? (3) What are current and future trends in preaching? The generative responses of both groups helped shape and clarify my thinking and the reader will notice, so much so, that the heart of the book is my response to the three questions. Let me give you a quick summary of the movements of the book.

Introduction to the Practice of African American Preaching opens with the first chapter: "The Bus Tour of the Study of African American Preaching."

---

4. Ibid., 11.

5. Donna E. Allen, *Toward a Womanist Homiletic: Katie Cannon, Alice Walker and Emancipatory Proclamation* (New York: Peter Lang Publishing, 2013), 8.

I will serve as your tour guide and explain how African American preaching has gradually moved from an almost exclusively oral to an oral/written tradition. A good tour guide knows how to interpret a site of learning; knows their history, geography, culture, and all the relevant facts; is filled with passion and excitement about the subject; presents information in a simple and precise way; and is an excellent storyteller and communicator. I hope that when the tour is concluded, you will gain tremendous insight into the history of the African American preaching tradition, and catch my enthusiasm, passion, and excitement for the tradition. In my travels, the best tour guides have left me wanting to return back to a site, and left me feeling as though I have made a new friend. I pray that it will be so when you conclude the introduction.

In the second chapter, "Negro Expression, Signifying, and the Rhetoric of African American Preaching," I discuss the fact that while there is a historical debate in European and Euro-American homiletical circles as to whether preaching is primarily a theological or rhetorical act, I argue that the oral traditions of West Africa and the brutal experience of slavery helped to shape what Zora Neale Hurston calls "Negro Expressions," and what Henry Louis Gates, the master trope of black rhetoric, calls "signifying." It is this unique construction of meaning through Negro expression and signifying that inherently joins the theological and rhetorical in African American preaching. I briefly trace the historical development of the relationship between homiletics and rhetoric in Western preaching, and then clarify that rhetoric is not an "add on" at the end of the sermon preparation process after we have figured out the theological content of the sermon. Rhetorical processes are central to the preaching process as well as theology and hermeneutics. In "Negro Expression," and African American preaching as part of Negro Expression, language is inherently rhetorical and theological.

The third chapter, "'It's Alright Now': A Rhetorical Analysis of Gardner C. Taylor's Sermon 'His Own Clothes,'" explores the question, "What is black preaching?" While typically this question is discussed in traditional theological and hermeneutical categories, the method of analysis herein is rhetorical criticism. I will briefly introduce the reader to methods of "close reading" and "ideological criticism." These methods form the heart of the rhetorical analysis of a sermon by Gardner Calvin Taylor, called the "Dean of Black Preaching," entitled "His Own Clothes," that is, a paradigmatic example of the highest and best of black preaching. We will discover that Taylor champions the gospel of Jesus Christ to victory, a victorious Christian people are formed and ready to act, and in the centuries-old healing words of the black church, "It's alright now."

The fourth chapter, "'Keepin' It Real': The Validity of the Existentially Authentic Performance," explores what is coined, from a rhetorical perspective, "communicative expression." Communicative expression is the belief that because the African American community blurs the lines between sacred and secular, it is important to study not only preachers and sermons inside the Christian church, but also whenever and wherever powerful oral communicative expression is uttered, whether it be in the church or in the culture, including literature, music, poetry, hip-hop, and so on. This chapter takes a cursory look at what lessons preaching can glean by examining the poetry of Jay-Z, a critically acclaimed representative of contemporary poetry in hip-hop music. From the perspective of hip-hop poetics and the validity of existential authentic performance, this chapter will consider this question: What is excellence in black preaching?

Chapter 5, "The Truth Is Always Relevant: Race and Economics in Contemporary African American Preaching," discusses the future trends in black preaching, specifically speaking to the question of the relevancy of the church to the African American Millennial generation. This article will explore how the church can engage, assist, and reach Millennials, who seek the reemergence of mass social justice movements. If the church does not address race and economics, or is not thoughtful and skilled in addressing these issues, Millennials will consider the church not relevant to their needs and struggles. Will the relevance of twenty-first-century sermons and churches be obvious and empowering to the mass social justice movements of today?

The final section of the book will be the afterword, and I am grateful that Jeremiah A. Wright Jr., pastor emeritus of Trinity United Church of Christ, preacher and scholar extraordinaire, will close the book with his lecture of his experience of "Seven Decades of African American Preaching." I could not think of a more fitting way to close *Introduction to the Practice of African American Preaching* than with a master practitioner of black preaching to offer us experience and historical survey of his seventy years as an African American preacher.

I once had a professor, John Angus Campbell, who called his Introduction to Rhetoric class "the Bus Tour." It was a marvelous metaphor for the class that presented the broad landscapes of the history of rhetorical thought and many exciting schools of rhetorical theory, rhetorical criticism, and rhetorical method. We strolled through historic times and places listening to great orators; found hidden gems of rhetorical wisdom and insight in the classics; took imaginary sunset cruises in discussion with Cicero, Aristotle, Augustine, and John Henry Newman; and laid on the beach with Kenneth Burke, Molefi Asante, and many others. The readings helped us come to understand that oratory is both a response to a rhetorical situation and how speakers creatively shaped arguments to persuade in that context. He was our academic tour guide who knew how to interpret a site of learning; knew geography, history, culture, and rhetorical facts; and was filled with passion and excitement about the subject. He was an excellent storyteller and communicator in that he modeled brilliant rhetorical skills in the presentation of the material. It was clear to us that he was thrilled that we had signed up for the tour. I caught his enthusiasm for the subject matter. It is my hope that you will surmise that I know how to interpret a site of learning, know my facts, am filled with passion, and am an excellent communicator. My hope is that you will catch my enthusiasm for the African American preaching tradition. As your tour guide, I am so excited that you have come along for the tour. I bid you welcome, as we open our discussion with the "Bus Tour" of the study of African American preaching.

Chapter One
THE BUS TOUR OF THE STUDY OF AFRICAN AMERICAN PREACHING

The quest for African American preaching to become a discipline in its own right continues a historical line of study of African American preaching. In order to fully appreciate this historical legacy, the first stop on our Bus Tour is to understand an important distinction in African American preaching that exists even to this day: the mutual and competing genres of "folk preaching" and "intellectual preaching." Basically, African American preachers operated from either a grassroots, folk approach ("old-time" and "old-fashioned Negro preaching") or an academic approach practiced primarily by preachers attending college and seminary (intellectual or educated preaching). The educated preaching tradition has left more written materials, while the folk tradition is primarily lodged in oral tradition. While these two traditions can often be at odds, many of the best of African American preachers were able to creatively combine elements of the best of both traditions, what Richard Lischer calls "theological erudition, with old-time religion."[1]

FOLK PREACHING AND EDUCATED PREACHING

African people were brought to America initially as indentured servants, but quickly and principally became racial slaves and human chattel,

---

1. Richard Lischer, *The Preacher King: Martin Luther King, Jr. and the Word That Moved America* (New York: Oxford University Press, 1995), 68.

experiencing what Orlando Patterson calls "social death."[2] The slave had no socially recognized existence outside of the master, and therefore became a social nonperson. The "natal alienation" of the socially dead person was expressed initially as being bereft of a soul, then once acknowledged as having a soul, not allowed to be baptized as a Christian because doing so could imply manumission. Despite their social death, African American religion existed and was initially practiced under slavery as "the invisible institution," mentioned by Albert J. Raboteau, consisting of secret and illegal gatherings for worship on plantations.[3] Many of these meetings were during the middle of the night in brush harbors, in barns, in fields, in gullies, under trees, and away from the purview of whites, and therefore considered relatively safe. Martha Simmons and I, in *Preaching with Sacred Fire: An Anthology of African American Preaching, from 1750 to the Present*, define the invisible institution as

> blacks participating in social and religious practices from preaching to conjuring to rebellion-hatching, to mourning, to moaning, to calling on Jesus. . . . This invisible institution existed alongside the churches that blacks attended with whites and alongside the gospel that was preached by whites who advocated submission and docility. Later it continued to exist alongside church formed by blacks and for blacks that began with white preachers, and those black churches that were more attentive to the espousal of white social and biblical doctrines than they were to black liberation.[4]

The style of worship was traditionally African with "shouts," "ring dancing," hand-clapping, and ecstatic expressions and utterances and led by one of their own. Therefore, the invisible institution generated the first African American leadership and for our purposes, the first African American preachers.

---

2. Orlando Patterson, *Slavery and Social Death: A Comparative Study* (Cambridge: Harvard University Press, 1982).

3. Albert Raboteau, *Slave Religion: The Invisible Institution in the Antebellum South* (New York: Oxford University Press, 2004).

4. Martha Simmons and Frank A. Thomas, *Preaching with Sacred Fire: An Anthology of African American Preaching, from 1750 to the Present* (New York: W. W. Norton, 2010), 22–23.

The majority of African American slaves did not become Christians until after the second decade of the nineteenth century, which many scholars attribute to the emotional means of evangelization of the Second Great Awakening. For some slaves and free persons of color, especially in the Methodist and Baptist persuasion, this emotional evangelization signified a bridge of commonality Christianity had with African Traditional Religion and they joined the Christian church in huge numbers. In Methodist revival services, where blacks and whites were allowed to participate together, passion ruled the day over doctrine. Indicative of this evangelism, Stephen H. Webb suggests:

> Weeping, shouting, and groaning were common at these services, although the emphasis was on deliverance from sin and the joyful experience of salvation.... [Blacks] were also inspired by the strong stand the Methodist leadership, following the guidance of Wesley himself, took against slavery. The Methodist message of personal holiness cut across racial, social, and economic lines, and a few of the most gifted blacks who joined the movement were encouraged to become preachers.[5]

One of these gifted black preachers was the well-known and widely traveled Black Harry (Harry Hoosier, d. 1810). He was a servant of the Methodist Bishop Asbury, and reputed by some to be the "greatest preacher in America," and drew large crowds of blacks and whites.

After being evangelized, black Christians were included as second-class Christians in white congregations, while some even branched out and formed their own churches. Free blacks in the North founded African American denominations, while large congregations in the South composed largely of enslaved blacks. The common denominator was that black preachers preached in all of these expressions of the church. What can be said from the earliest times, starting with the invisible institution, black preachers and black preaching existed, and so did the division between folk preaching and intellectual preaching, highly influenced by freedom related to geography and social status.

---

5. Stephen H. Webb, "Introducing Black Harry Hoosier: The History behind Indiana's Namesake," scholarworks.iu.edu/journals/index.php/imh/article/view/11895/17497, accessed February 8, 2016.

Chapter One

Intellectual preaching came from mostly the North, done by blacks who either were born free or purchased their freedom (freedmen), and had gained access to education, such as Lemuel Haynes, John Chavis, Absalom Jones, and Hosea Easton. In the nineteenth century, Richard Allen, father of the first independent African denomination in the United States, the African Methodist Episcopal Church, and Rev. Andrew Marshall, pastor of the First African Baptist Church in Savannah, Georgia, preached to large numbers of blacks and whites. Many of these preachers followed the form and structure of Euro-American preaching with the propositional nature of deductive reasoning as the argumentation structure of the sermon and classical rhetorical tenets, modes, and methods of persuasion as the basis of the homiletical preparation and delivery. Preaching in this educated strand was didactic and centered in formal language, usually addressing erudite theological issues. O. C. Edwards, in *A History of Preaching*, explains one of the critical goals of educated preachers: "to show that members of their race were as intellectually capable as whites, and that they could produce sermons that were as eloquent and closely argued as the best white preaching of the time."[6] As a result, the educated preaching tradition sought to distinguish itself from folk preaching, too often regarding it as undignified, emotional, illiterate, buffoonery, and embarrassing.

Folk preachers, by contrast, represented preachers without formal education and include Brother Carper, Gullah Negro preacher Brudder Coteney, John Jasper, and Sojourner Truth, from the earliest periods of African American preaching, 1750–1865.[7] Walter Pitts provides clarity on the black folk preacher and sermon: "The term *black folk sermon* refers to the Sunday verbal performance of the black folk preacher who is not seminary-trained but called to the ministry by some visionary experience and whose congregation consists principally of black working-class worshipers [the folk]."[8] The oral tradition of folk preaching affirmed the

---

6. O. C. Edwards, *A History of Preaching* (Nashville: Abingdon Press, 2004), 530.

7. See "Brudder Coteney's Sermons," Gullah Negro sermons edited by John G. Williams, *De Ole Plantation* (Charleston, SC: Walker, Evans, & Cogswell, 1895) and William E. Hatcher, *John Jasper* (New York: F. H. Revell, 1908).

8. Walter Pitts, "West African Poetics in the Black Preaching Style," *American Speech* 64 (Summer 1989): 137.

power of story, imagination, imagery, analogy, metaphor, narration, and extemporaneous and dramatic retellings of Bible stories. Intonation, or "whooping," is one of the common hallmarks of the folk-preaching tradition. Whooping is the rhetorical practice, traditionally at the end of the sermon, in which the preacher sings or chants in rhythmic cadence in the vernacular of call and response that raises the emotional intensity and impact of the sermon.[9] Speaking specifically of folk preachers on phonograph records in the twentieth-century interwar period, but true generally for all folk preachers, Lerone A. Martin comments:

> Their [folk] preaching was marked by metaphor, simile, double descriptors (high-tall, low-down, kill-dead, more-better) and the use of verbal nouns such as "funeralize." The sermons were also chanted, beginning with conversational prose and then transitioning to a "metrical, tonal, and rhythmic chant." . . . Moreover, these antiphonal sermons avoided scholarly theological discourse. Instead, they employed black dialect, idioms, and memes to preach on topics such as Christian piety, racism, and popular cultural events: everyday black life.[10]

While such preachers probably did not formally know the tenets of Western rhetoric, they employed many of the same rhetorical communication strategies, and therefore, rhetoric, broadly conceived, can help describe what happens in the folk sermon tradition. Several chroniclers of the African American tradition have applied Cicero's five canons of rhetoric (invention, arrangement, style, memory, and delivery) and Aristotle's modes of persuasion (ethos, logos, and pathos) to African American preaching, but more about the rhetorical nature of African American preaching later. With this important distinction of folk/educated preaching clarified, I want to make the second stop on the Bus Tour of the historical development of the study of African American preaching, the paucity of the academic study of African American preaching.

---

9. See Martha Simmons's article "Whooping: The Musicality of African American Preaching Past and Present," in Simmons and Thomas, *Preaching with Sacred Fire*, 865–84. Whooping is also referred to as intoning, chanting, moaning, and tuning, and these terms will be used interchangeably throughout the book.

10. Lerone A. Martin, *Preaching on Wax: The Phonograph and the Shaping of Modern African American Religion* (New York: New York University Press, 2014), 93.

CHAPTER ONE

THE PAUCITY OF ACADEMIC STUDY OF AFRICAN AMERICAN PREACHING

While there are many chronicled sermons and much commentary about black preaching in slave narratives and American religious and social history, the academic study of the homiletic methods of the African American preaching tradition, until the early 1970s, was minimal. It was not that sermons were not published, but few sermons entered academic and scholarly literature. Gerald L. Davis comments:

> Most African American churches found the occasion to publish one or a set of sermons, frequently on the occasion of an anniversary. The archival collections held in the libraries of Fisk and Howard Universities and other African American institutions, the Library of Congress, in New York Public Library and other university and municipal libraries around the nation include a number of significant and historically important sermons "published" by African American preachers and their congregations.[11]

While African American churches and preachers published their sermons, O. C. Edwards labels the emergence of African American preaching in majority and academic consciousness as a "homiletical epiphany":

> Among the many streams of tradition that converged to form late-twentieth-century understanding of the nature of preaching, none showed the proclaimed word's potentialities to move people and change society as did the classical homiletic of the African American church. As much as its pulpit had done to sustain its people through slavery, reconstruction, and segregation, it was hardly known to the rest of American society until the civil rights movement got underway in the late-1950s. Then, however, it burst on the national scene with dazzling brightness.[12]

There are at least four principal reasons for this significant omission of scholarship: (1) much of the genius of African American preaching traveled in oral tradition, (2) black homiletics, for the most part, was passed

---

11. Gerald L. Davis, *I Got the Word in Me, and I Can Sing It, You Know: A Study of the Performed African American Sermon* (Philadelphia: University of Philadelphia Press, 1985), 40.

12. Edwards, *A History of Preaching*, 703.

on in the apprenticeship model of the black church, (3) based upon Western intellectual bias, few scholars paid serious attention to the complexity of African American preaching, and (4) until the 1970s African American preaching was primarily studied by nontheological and few homiletical scholars.

First, much of the genius of the folk tradition of African American preaching tradition has been oral, and as such, traveled for years in the oral tradition. The drawback to this oral tradition has been that some of the best of African American preaching has gone to the grave with preachers because much of that genius was not captured, written down, or archived. Or, if it was written down, it was not accessible to the wider community because it was stored in church basements; in personal, denominational, and convention archives, newspapers, pamphlets, and the like; or in the hands of family members. Again, it is here that one of the main reasons for my vision of African American preaching as an academic discipline locates itself: the need for scholars to capture, archive, research, and publish the genius of this oral tradition that is potentially diminishing as I write this sentence. Not only is black preaching lessened, but all traditions of preaching are diminished by the loss of these treasured resources that travel almost exclusively in the oral tradition.

Second, connected to the oral folk tradition of black preaching, homiletical theory and method was passed on in the apprenticeship model of the black church, where primarily one learns to preach through observation, study, and imitation of models.[13] Every preaching tradition, including African American preaching, has models that because of their excellence in manifesting the tradition are considered to be worthy of imitation. In the African American preaching tradition, performers of the tradition observe and learn directly from these models more than

---

13. For more detailed information on the apprenticeship model of African American preaching, please see Frank A. Thomas, *They Like to Never Quit Praisin' God: The Role of Celebration in Preaching*, 2nd ed. (Cleveland, OH: Pilgrim Press, 2013), 5–9 and Dale P. Andrew's two-part article on the apprenticeship model and the teaching of black preaching in "Teaching Black Preaching: Encounter and Re-encounter," *The African American Pulpit* 9, no. 4 (Fall 2006): 8–12, "Teaching Black Preaching: Homiletic Instruction as 'Pre-Encounter,'" *The African American Pulpit* 10, no. 1 (Winter, 2006–2007): 22–26.

the application of rules or homiletical textbooks. There are few explicit written rules per se, but a multitude of lived practices represented by the models. In oral tradition, models are more important than written rules and textbooks. For example, Jesse Louis Jackson said that C. L. Franklin was "the most imitated soul preacher in history."[14] As part of oral culture, Franklin made significant inroads into the black community through proliferation of sermons on radio stations, travel preaching tours, and phonograph records, which facilitated his imitation in the observation, study, and practice of the apprenticeship model of the oral tradition of African American preaching.

Third, as part of the apprentice model for those to whom formal education was not available, accessible, or affordable, the educational and skill development choice was also denominational meetings and institutes.[15] It was at these gatherings that many got exposure to the aforementioned models. These conferences provided teaching, training, lectures, instruction, and workshops in Bible, theology, ethics, hermeneutics, and preaching, as well as much needed spiritual inspiration and fellowship. The Hampton University Ministers' Conference and Choir Directors' & Organists' Guild (Hampton) is the most distinguished historical and contemporary African American conference for the training of ministers, with thousands attending each June on the campus of Hampton University, Hampton, Virginia.[16] The conference began in 1914 and stated that the critical objective of the Ministers' Conference was "the promotion of the work of the Kingdom of God through study and discussion of those problems and tasks with which all ministers share in common." Training

---

14. Jeff Todd Titon, *Give Me This Mountain: Life History and Selected Sermons* (Urbana, IL: University of Illinois Press, 1989).

15. For more information on the education of black preachers, see "Education and Ministry," in Charles V. Hamilton, *The Black Preacher in America* (New York: William Morrow & Company, 1972), 84–109.

16. Besides Hampton University Ministers' Conference and Choir Directors' & Organists' Guild there are many historical and contemporary predominantly African American preaching institutes and conferences: Lacy Kirk Williams Institute http://lkwilliamsinstitute.org/index.html, E. K. Bailey Expository Preaching Conference http://ekbpc.com, The Charles E. Booth Preaching Conference, www.cebpreachingconference.com, The Gardner C. Taylor Distinguished Preaching Series, Voice of the Prophet Preaching Conference: Examining the Preaching of C. L. Franklin for a New Generation, www.voiceofaprophet.com.

and instruction was provided on "the problems and tasks with which all ministers share in common."[17] What distinguishes Hampton is the combination of the interdenominational nature of attendees and its attraction of folk and intellectual preachers.

Across the years, while continuing the focus on training, it was the distinguished preachers who were lifted up as the models worthy of imitation that fundamentally set the conference apart from all others. Preachers such as Sandy Ray, C. L Franklin, William Holmes Borders, Ella Mitchell, Vernon Johns, J. H. Jackson, Howard Thurman, Martin Luther King Jr., Benjamin E. Mays, Charles G. Adams, Prathia Hall, Jeremiah A. Wright Jr., and the list could go on and on. Hampton became known for the preaching going on there. Aside from the preaching, there were practical lectures and seminars, on church growth, Christian education, contemporary culture and trends, ministerial ethics, business practices of the church, and so forth. While there is not time on our tour to explore Hampton, this is a rich source of material for scholarship on African American preaching. It would be fruitful to study not only the sermons of Hampton but also the lectures on preaching done there. My hope is some future scholar would explore the depths of this preaching and homiletical instruction, not only at Hampton, but also at all of the historical and contemporary institutes and denominational assemblages.

Next, according to Gerald L. Davis, few scholars "have fully appreciated the complexity of the structures of the performed African American sermon."[18] Few scholars treat "the performed African American sermon as a unified system of sociosemantic structures." Davis gives three basic reasons for this underestimation and underreporting of the African American sermon. First, many scholars were distrustful of the high emotionalism of the African American sermon, equating such with a lack of sophistication and education. Second, closely tied to the first, is the belief that "rationality is inversely proportional to the presence of emotionalism in the church

---

17. Timothy Tee Boddie, "The Future of the Hampton University Ministers' Conference," *The African American Pulpit, The Best of the Hampton Ministers' Conference* 5, no. 2 (Spring 2002): 17.

18. Gerald L. Davis, *I Got the Word in Me and I Can Sing It, You Know*, 39.

and the academic training of the preacher."[19] Third, connected to the first two, is that the overarching belief was that the performed African American sermon was not based in reasoned philosophical sensibilities. Davis argues that preaching performances in African American churches tend to be "densely layered" and conventional research approaches might be inadequate to understand the rhetorical, cultural, and religious dynamics involved. As evidence of this, scholars were ignorant of the fact and possibility that a preacher can be learned and emotional at the same time. And last, the African American–performed sermon is fully reasoned and philosophic. There is without a shadow of doubt, from the structural level, rhetorical theory and method, including "aesthetic dimensions" and "organizing principles" that guide and direct the performed African American sermon.

Finally, until the early 1970s, African American preaching was primarily studied by scholars of folklore, public address, anthropology, social science, history, ethnomusicology, rhetoric, and a host of related disciplines and subdisciplines that focus on language in culture and society rather than scholars of religion and homiletics. While many of these scholars made a significant contribution to the body of knowledge around the African American sermon, homiletical inquiry and methodology was not their main focus. It was not until the work of Henry H. Mitchell in the latter part of the twentieth century that the academic field of homiletics paid much attention to black preaching. Let us now move to the third stop on the Bus Tour of the study of African American preaching, the study of African American preaching before Martin Luther King Jr.

THE STUDY OF AFRICAN AMERICAN PREACHING BEFORE MARTIN LUTHER KING JR.

While much of the homiletic method of African American preaching traveled in oral tradition and mentorship models of the African American community, in 1903, W. E. B. DuBois published the American classic *The Souls of Black Folk*, consisting of a collection of thirteen essays and one short story written between 1897 and 1903. According to David

---

19. Ibid., 41.

W. Blight and Robert Gooding-Williams, *Souls* was written to "explore the 'strange meaning of being black' in a society that viewed blacks with contempt."[20] DuBois details African American social and spiritual life, struggle for civil rights, economic and social legacies of slavery, and the contribution of blacks to the American identity in the attempt to unseat prejudice in American life, "hoping fervently to create a society in which it would no longer hold sway."[21] DuBois does not give much attention to the sermons of preachers, but he does record this statement that reflects the importance of the Negro preacher and their sermons to the African American community:

> The Preacher is the most unique personality developed by the Negro on American soil. A leader, a politician, an orator, a "boss" an intriguer, and idealist.... The combination of certain adroitness with deep-seated earnestness, of tact with consummate ability, gave him his preeminence, and helps him maintain it.[22]

Following DuBois, Carter G. Woodson in *The History of the Negro Church* traces the influence of the black church from colonial times to the early years of the twentieth century.[23] Woodson viewed ministry as one of the highest positions to which a black leader could aspire based upon access to education and visibility. To augment this view, Woodson includes short biographies of preachers who were instrumental in the development and growth of the Negro church, but does little with their sermons or homiletical methods. Benjamin E. Mays and Joseph William Nicholson also published a comprehensive study of the Negro church.[24] Their purpose was to give an "accurate description of the Negro Church

---

20. W. E. B. Dubois, *The Souls of Black Folk*, ed. David. W. Blight and Robert Gooding-Williams (New York: Bedford Books, 1997).

21. Ibid., 2.

22. Ibid., 149.

23. Carter G. Woodson, *The History of the Negro Church*, 2nd ed. (Washington, DC: The Associated Publishers, 1921).

24. Benjamin Elijah Mays and Joseph William Nicholson, "The Negro's Church" (New York: Aron Press & New York Times, 1969), originally published in 1933 by the Institute of Social and Religious Research, New York.

in America," studying 609 urban and 185 rural churches in twelve cities and four counties. One chapter of the study is entitled "Message of the Minister," and is dedicated to the thought content of the sermons of black preachers. Mays and Nicholson note that the church is the chief place where Negroes are stimulated "emotionally and intellectually," and their purpose was to examine what congregants were being taught from the pulpit. Collecting one hundred sermons, they divided them into three classes: those that (1) touch life situations, (2) are doctrinal or theological, (3) and are predominately otherworldly. Mays and Nicholson close the chapter by making several conclusions about the content of the sermons, such as making judgments on the God idea, appealing to the emotions of hearers versus appealing to their intellect, and the characteristics of otherworldly preaching versus preaching that speaks to the social and economic issues that confront the Negro.

Two of the better-known chroniclers of African American folk preaching are Zora Neale Hurston and James Weldon Johnson. Both based their findings on interviews with preachers or hearing and recording sermons preached in authentic folk settings. Hurston used her talents as a writer, trained anthropologist, and folklorist to distinctively capture the diversities of black culture and folklore in the United States as well as in Bermuda, Haiti, and Jamaica. In Florida, about 1918, she recorded a classic example of folk preaching at its best in the sermon of C. C. Lovelace, entitled "The Wounds of Jesus."[25] We will have more discussion of Hurston in the next chapter when we examine her important work on "Negro Expression."

In 1927, James Weldon Johnson's poetic renditions of African American folk sermons of the old-time Negro preacher appeared in *God's Trombones* and became an instant classic.[26] Johnson states that his purpose for publishing the book is that the old-time Negro preacher has not been given their due and proper respect. He affirms with DuBois, Mays and Nicholson, and Woodson, the important role of the black preacher and

---

25. Zora Neale Hurston, *The Sanctified Church* (Berkeley, CA: Turtle Island Press, 1981).

26. James Weldon Johnson, *God's Trombones* (New York: Penguin Books, 2008), original (New York: Viking Press, 1927).

adds that though the power of the old-time preacher has "somewhat lessened and changed in his successors . . . in fact, it is still the greatest single influence among the colored people of the United States. The Negro today is, perhaps, the most priest-governed group in the country."[27]

Johnson also recounts the rhetorical effect and power of the preacher, but again does little homiletical analysis. As an example of Johnson's descriptive analysis, he records the story of a famed preacher he once heard who was losing his audience to boredom, and suddenly, he closed the Bible, stepped from behind the pulpit, and began to preach. He intoned an old folk-sermon beginning with creation and ending with Judgment Day. Johnson comments:

> He was at once a changed man, free, at ease and masterful. . . . An electric current ran through the crowd. . . . It was in a moment alive and quivering. . . . He was wonderful in the way he employed his conscious and unconscious art. He strode the pulpit up and down in what was actually a very rhythmic dance, and he brought into play the full gamut of his wonderful voice, a voice—what shall I say?—not of an organ or a trumpet, but rather of a trombone, the instrument possessing above all others the power to express the wide and varied range of emotions encompassed by the human voice—and with greater amplitude.[28]

The old-time Negro preacher was God's trombone, and according to Johnson, "the old-time Negro preacher is rapidly passing away" as black preaching became more educated and less emotional.[29]

William Pipes continues an important discussion of "Old Time Negro Preaching" in 1951.[30] Pipes defines two important periods of old-time Negro preaching:

> Old-time Negro preaching existed during slavery from 1732 (the period of the great influence of Whitefield's preaching upon Negro slaves) until

---

27. Ibid., 2.
28. Ibid., 5–6.
29. Ibid., 8.
30. William Pipes, *Say Amen Brother: A Study in American Frustration* (Westport, CT: Negro Universities Press, 1951).

1832 (the period of reaction against Negro preaching, following Nat Turner's slave insurrection.) From this hundred year era until the present time [1951], Negro preaching has been undergoing a change; however, some of the original characteristics and manifestations [emotional] are to be found, in varying degrees, in Negro preaching today.[31]

Fearing old-time Negro preaching was passing away, Pipes's purpose was to offer an interpretive study based upon recordings of seven sermons from Macon County, Georgia, and concludes that old-time Negro preaching unknowingly observes many of the traditions of rhetoric. Pipes does an analysis of old-time Negro preaching according to four of Cicero's classical five constituents of rhetoric (invention, disposition, style, and delivery) and Aristotle's three modes of persuasion (ethos, pathos, and logos).

Pipes suggests the major rhetorical or persuasive challenge, or rhetorical situation, of the old-time Negro preachers and how it was solved:

> His preaching [old-time Negro preacher], for sure, is unique. He must interest his hearers, but he must not mention their most vital problem: white supremacy in the South. Therefore, the Negro minister appeals mainly to the emotions of his audience and leads his hearers to thinking primarily of things of the world which is to come after death, "for God's Got the World in His Hands." [32]

The basic thrust of what Pipes suggests as "thinking primarily of things of the world which is to come after death," is true, and it is also true that much old-time Negro preaching was more nuanced, having shades of the tradition of double meaning contained in the spirituals and a regular part of black communication as we will discuss in the next chapter. While speaking to "over yonder," the preachers also spoke to concrete liberation realities in the present world here and now.

African American preachers have always had the challenge of confronting the reality of white supremacy, and by and large, great amounts

---

31. Ibid., 7.
32. Ibid., 2.

of racial indifference.[33] This reality is still true in the present moment. Without a viable option of armed violence and revolution to secure human dignity and freedom, the black community has had to rely upon persuasion in its many forms (i.e., nonviolent protest, boycotts, sit-ins, legal remedies, community organizing, voting, speeches and sermons of inspiration, moral suasion, and such). The truth of Pipes's statement is still relevant: the persuasive task of the African American preacher is to interest their hearers and speak to the basic reality that the daily existence of black people must be lived in an often hostile world dominated by structures of white supremacy, which is like, as O. C. Edwards advocates, "living with a hatchet over your head every day."[34]

Bruce Rosenberg, in *Can These Bones Live? The Art of the American Folk Preacher*, analyzes the African American chanted sermon from the perspective of Albert B. Lord's epic theory of oral composition. According to Lord, the oral composition of African American folk preaching tradition had evolved to the extent that it paralleled the folklore and epic poetry of other continents and centuries, going as far back as *Beowulf*.[35]

---

33. I use the term *white supremacist* in the same manner as Thomas Kane, who says, "By *white supremacist*, I don't mean to suggest that the entire nation is wearing Klan gear or painting graffiti swastikas; instead, I intend the term to connote a *de facto* white supremacy, where the privilege of whiteness is assumed and perpetuated across generations so that taking the historically long view, the majority of property, wealth, and material goods are owned and operated for white profit. This inequality is embedded in our society by generations of choosing the comfort of apathy over genuine challenge of equality—material, political, rhetorical, and representational" (Thomas Kane, "Bringing the Real: Lacan and Tupac," in *Prospects: An Annual of American Cultural Studies*, ed. Jack Salzman, Cambridge University Press, Volume 27 (2002): 641–663, at 661). I add that choosing the comfort of apathy over the genuine challenge of equality is racial indifference. Michele Alexander defines racial indifference as "a lack of compassion and caring about race and racial groups." It is different than racial hostility where the assumption that systems are "necessarily predicated on the desire to harm other racial groups." (See Michele Alexander, *The New Jim Crow: Mass Incarceration in the Age of Colorblindness* [New York: The New Press, 2010], 203).

34. The phrase "living with a hatchet over your head every day" is quoted in O. C. Edwards, *A History of Preaching*, 544.

35. Bruce Rosenberg, *Can These Bones Live? The Art of the American Folk Preacher*, rev. ed. (Urbana, IL: University of Illinois, 1970).

Rosenberg's work engaged scholarly conversation, and several other folklorists began to analyze the African American folk sermon. [36]

In the tradition of DuBois, Woodson, Mays, and Nicholson, in 1972, Charles V. Hamilton published *The Black Preacher in America*, and argued that "the black preacher, has been, and remains, one of the most praised and condemned persons in American society. Comments about him run the spectrum from 'jackleg' to hustler to statesman, to 'man of God,' and include every conceivable indictment and award society has to offer."[37]

Since black people were brought to the country as indentured servants and slaves, the black preacher was the spokesperson and therefore an important person in the lives of black people. Hamilton seeks to look at the fundamental ways the black preacher has been important by discussing the many roles of the black preacher in the church and the community, the black preacher's relationship to black people, the role of the minister during slavery, number and distribution of black churches, the ministers' relationship to politics, and so on. He does not, however, discuss their preaching, or the role of preaching, and while generally very useful, despite the exclusion of women preachers, his book is not helpful to our homiletical concerns.

One of the most significant contributions by folklorists concerned with the chanted sermon is Gerald L. Davis's *I Got the Word in Me and I Can Sing It, You Know: A Study of the Performed African American Sermon*.[38] Davis seeks to answer this question: How does one know when a

---

36. See Roger Abrahams, *Deep Down in the Jungle: Negro Narrative Folklore from the Streets of Philadelphia* (Chicago: Aldine, 1970); William Clements and Stephen Glazer, *Marchin' the Pilgrims Home: Leadership and Decision-Making in an Afro-Caribbean Faith* (Oxford: Greenwood Press, 1984); Gary Layne Hatch, "Logic in the Black Folk Sermon: The Sermons of Rev. C. L. Franklin," *Journal of Black Studies* 26 (January 1996): 227–44; Lyndrey A. Niles, "Rhetorical Characteristics of Traditional Black Preaching," *Journal of Black Studies* 15 (September 1984): 41–52; Catherine Peck, "Your Daughters Shall Prophesy: Women in the Afro-American Preaching Tradition," (master's thesis, University of North Carolina, 1983); Richard L. Wright, "Language Standards and Communicative Style in the Black Church" (PhD diss., University of Texas at Austin, 1976).

37. Charles V. Hamilton, *The Black Preacher in America* (New York: William Morrow & Company, 1972), 3.

38. Gerald L. Davis, *I Got the Word in Me and I Can Sing It, You Know*.

performed African American sermon is "good"? He develops a model for the testing of the African American–performed sermon and how to conclude whether it is good or successful:

> The well-preached sermon fully develops its constituent formulas and formulaic structures. Metaphorical images are fully drawn. Bible verses are stated and interpreted, ideas are presented abstractly and applied concretely, exempla and other generic forms are used as full sequences in the sermon, and the preacher moves progressively from one formula to the next through transitional free clauses.[39]

Jon Michael Spencer, in his book *Sacred Symphony: The Chanted Sermon of the Black Preacher*, offers tremendous insights into the musicality of the chanted sermon by making the clear connection between the chanted sermons of contemporary black preachers and the antebellum spiritual. Spencer argues that "a substantial quantum of spirituals evolved via the preaching event of black worship," and as a result delineates common musical components of the chanted sermon and the spiritual—melody, rhythm, call and response, counterpoint, harmony, form, and improvisation.[40] William C. Turner highlights the value of the book when he says, "The persistence and pervasiveness of musicality in black preaching is intriguing when one considers the paucity of reflection upon the idiom."[41]

It is impossible in any study of African American religion for any discipline to not mention the landmark work of C. Eric Lincoln's and Lawrence H. Mamiya's *The Black Church in the African American Experience*, the largest nongovernmental survey of the urban and rural black church resulting in a comprehensive sociological study of the black church combining a comprehensive historical overview of seven mainline black denominations.[42] Lincoln and Mamiya do not spend much time on African American preaching other than to acknowledge preaching as the

---

39. Ibid.

40. Jon Michael Spencer, *Sacred Symphony: The Chanted Sermon of the Black Preacher* (New York: Greenwood Press, 1987), xiii.

41. Ibid., ix.

42. C. Eric Lincoln and Lawrence H. Mamiya, *The Black Church in the African American Experience* (Durham, NC: Duke University Press, 1990).

focal point of black worship and, like Jon Michael Spencer, its connection to the powerful musical traditions in the African American church, including spirituals, hymn-lining, meter music, "the golden age of gospel," contemporary gospel music, and music of the civil rights and freedom movements.

The aforementioned quote by Jesse Louis Jackson referring to C. L. Franklin as the most imitated black preacher in history was published in Jeff Todd Titon's *Give Me This Mountain: Life History and Selected Sermons of C. L. Franklin*. Titon offers highlights from Franklin's life history and twenty of his best sermons based upon thirty hours of tape-recorded conversations and twenty-two video recordings of Franklin's sermons preached in the sanctuary of New Bethel Baptist Church of Detroit, Michigan, from 1976 to 1978.[43] Titon provides these sermons in written text "in the hope that the African American sermon will take its rightful place in the American literary canon."[44] Titon projects that at some point in the future seventy-five of Franklin's sermons will appear in a volume of a larger work.

The study of the African American folk sermon continued to widen as ethnographers and ethnomusicologists began to explore the claim that the artistry of the African American folk sermon goes back to West Africa.[45] Again, as evidence of and testimony to the power of the African American sermon in African American life, English and African American studies professor Dolan Hubbard argues that African American writers, such as Zora Neale Hurston, Ralph Ellison, James Baldwin, and Toni Morrison, "use the rhetorical forms of the black preaching style, with its attendant expressive power, to bring readers to the point of recognizing their characters' symbolic importance."[46] Finally, Lerone A. Martin, in *Preaching*

---

43. Jeff Todd Titon, *Give Me This Mountain: Life History and Selected Sermons*.

44. Ibid., 42.

45. See Pitts, "West African Poetics Black Preaching Style"; Joyce Jackson, "The Black American Folk Preacher and the Chanted Sermon: Parallels with a West African Tradition," in *Discourse in Ethnomusicology II: A Tribute to Alan Merriam*, ed. Caroline Card, Jane Cowan, Sally Carr Helton, et. al.. (Bloomington, IN: Ethnomusicology Publications Group, 1981), 205–22.

46. Dolan Hubbard, *The Sermon and the African American Literary Imagination* (Colombia, MO: University of Missouri Press, 1994), 21.

on Wax: The Phonograph and the Shaping of Modern African American Religion, describes how African American ministers, such as the Reverend J. M. Gates, during the period of 1926–1941 teamed up with major phonograph labels to sell and market their sermons to an enthusiastic black consumer market. Martin successfully argues that this "phonograph religion" significantly shaped modern African American Christianity. [47]Martin is the latest in a long and continuing lineage of scholars outside of the field of homiletics that make major contributions to ascertaining how the black sermon as a cultural and religious phenomenon has influenced American life.[48] The fourth stop on our Bus Tour is the study of African American preaching by the field of homiletics after the death of Martin Luther King Jr.

THE STUDY OF AFRICAN AMERICAN PREACHING AFTER MARTIN LUTHER KING JR.

In the preaching of Martin Luther King Jr. (1955–68) and several other well-known African American preachers of the civil rights movement, the folk and educated strands of African American preaching converged and majority America had a "homiletical epiphany" and became aware of the power of black preaching.[49] Mervyn Warren, in his book *King Came Preaching: The Pulpit Power of Dr. Martin Luther King Jr.*, suggests:

> So it was not only happenstance that preaching by African Americans began receiving serious and sustained formal hearing in homiletic hallways only in the early or middle 1970s, as we settled to live with King's absence and realize the eternal effect of his preaching ministry on all facets of our lives. In fact, the increased visibility and respectability of

---

47. Lerone A. Martin, *Preaching on Wax: The Phonograph and the Shaping of Modern African American Religion*.

48. See Roxanne Mountford, *The Gendered Pulpit: Preaching in American Protestant Spaces* (Carbondale, IL: Southern University Press, 2003); Nick Salvatore, *Singing in a Strange Land: C. L. Franklin, the Black Church, and the Transformation of America* (New York: Little, Brown and Company, 2005); Cheryl Wharry, *Amen and Hallelujah Preaching: Discourse Functions in African American Sermons* (Cambridge: Cambridge University Press, 2003).

49. King was surrounded by gifted preachers and might not have been the best preacher among them, including Prathia Hall, Joseph Lowry, Andrew Young, Walter Fauntroy, Jesse Jackson, C. T. Vivian, Ralph Abernathy, and others. There were other civil rights campaigns with clergy doing additional and complimentary work, but the media focused on King.

black preaching in America can be split into two distinct eras, B.K. and A.K.—Before King and After King.[50]

The reader can recognize that I agree with Warren's assessment, as I have labeled two important sections of this chapter as having to do with before King and after King. King was squarely located in the educated strand of African American preaching, following in the footsteps of Mordecai Wyatt Johnson, Benjamin Elijah Mays, and Vernon Johns. Though not considered a folk preacher, King borrowed heavily from folk preachers, including his father, grandfather, and many African American preachers he heard growing up and with whom he worked in the civil rights movement. King merged parts of liberal white (Fosdick, Hamilton, Bosely) and African American intellectual and educated preaching traditions (Johnson, Mays, Johns) with African American (many unnamed and illiterate) folk preaching traditions to create a discourse that spoke to most Americans and contributed to significant social change in America.[51]

There was scholarship on the African American sermon prior to 1968, but after the death of King that scholarship expanded significantly. The iconic stature and respect given the oratory of King in American culture ignited scholarly interest and passion in the study of African American preaching. The noted homiletical scholar Richard L. Eslinger attributes the civil rights movement as one of the forces that contributed to the "New Homiletic" of Euro-American preaching in the 1970s and 1980s that he chronicles:

> For many majority-culture Christians, the first significant encounter with African American preaching occurred during the civil right struggles of the 1950s and '60s. A number of us returned from these profound and moving experiences to our pastorates or to seminary never to be the same. Among the myriad of memories to be sorted out were

---

50. Mervyn Warren, *King Came Preaching: The Pulpit Power of Dr. Martin Luther King Jr.* (Downers Grove, IL: InterVarsity Press, 2001), 52.

51. See Keith D. Miller, *Voice of Deliverance: The Language of Martin Luther King Jr. and Its Sources* (New York: The Free Press, 1992).

worship services of fervent prayer and praise and preaching at once prophetic and pastoral and celebratory. [52]

To put it simply, after listening to King and so many others, mainstream America paid much more attention to the African American preaching tradition, and scholarship, such as in the fields of rhetoric and theology, followed as a part of this interest. Rhetorical scholars analyzed King's speeches and sermons, such as "Letter from a Birmingham Jail," "I Have a Dream," and "I've Been to the Mountaintop."[53] In addition to King and civil rights preachers, scholars began to pay attention to Malcolm X and others of the Black Nationalist persuasion, historical and contemporary figures such as Frederick Douglass, Ida B. Wells, W. E. B. DuBois, Adam Clayton Powell Jr., Mary McCloud Bethune, Barbara Jordan, and others.

In the publishing of *Black Theology and Black Power* (1969) and *A Black Theology of Liberation* (1970), James H. Cone established a groundbreaking marker in the academy by articulating theology from the African American perspective.[54] It is important to highlight in brief the importance of Cone, who, as L. Susan Bond says, "is a watershed figure, not only for theological education concerns but for our current consideration of the leadership styles and assumptions of a new era of African American homileticians."[55] In the first two-thirds of the twentieth century, the key tenor for African American religious life was (1) social conformity based upon the black mass migration from the South to the North and the

---

52. O. Wesley Allen, Jr., ed. *The Renewed Homiletic* (Minneapolis: Fortress Press, 2010), 128.

53. See *Martin Luther King Jr. and the Sermonic Power of Public Discourse*, eds. Carolyn Calloway-Thomas and John Louis Lucaites (Tuscaloosa: University of Alabama Press, 1993); Keith D. Miller, *Martin Luther King's Biblical Epic: His Final, Great Speech* (Jackson: University of Mississippi Press, 2012); Fredrik Sunnemark, *Ring Out Freedom: The Voice of Martin Luther King Jr. and the Making of the Civil Rights Movement* (Bloomington, IN: Indiana University Press, 2004).

54. James H. Cone, *Black Theology and Black Power* (New York: Seabury Press, 1969) and *A Black Theology of Liberation* (Philadelphia: J. B. Lipincott, 1970).

55. L. Susan Bond, *Contemporary African American Preaching: Diversity in Theory and Style* (St. Louis: Chalice Press, 2003).

church's attempt to help these new pilgrims adjust to urban realities,[56] and (2) the civil rights movement that principally was committed to integration, democracy, and inclusion of African Americans into the "American Dream." Radicalism mostly came from outside the church, from, for example, Marcus Garvey, the Student Non-violent Coordinating Committee, Elijah Muhammad and the Nation of Islam, Molefi Asante, and Malcolm X. While there have always been strands of social protest in the form of Christian radicalism in African American preaching, particularly in the nineteenth century, such as Henry McNeal Turner, Henry Highland Garnett, Martin Delaney, Frances Ellen Watkins, Ida B. Wells, Anna Julia Cooper, and Alexander Crummell, during the late 1960s and early 1970s Christian radicalism gave rise to Afrocentric and African-centered thought, such as Albert B. Cleage Jr. (Jaramogi Abebe Agyeman), who founded the Shrine of the Black Madonna, in Detroit, Michigan (1970), and Jeremiah A. Wright Jr., who became the pastor of Trinity United Church of Christ of Chicago, Illinois (1972), which earlier had announced itself as "unashamedly black and unapologetically Christian."[57] As part of the milieu, Cone ignited contemporary Christian radicalism in academic theological circles by accommodating African American Christianity and the black power movements to inaugurate black theology.

---

56. See Kenyatta R. Gilbert, *A Pursued Justice: Black Preaching from the Great Migration to Civil Rights* (Waco, TX: Baylor University Press, 2016). Gilbert argues that in the wake of a failed Reconstruction period, widespread agricultural depression, and the rise of Jim Crow laws, and triggered by America's entry into World War I, a flood of southern blacks moved from the South to the urban centers of the North. This Great Migration transformed northern black churches and produced a new mode of preaching—prophetic black preaching—which sought to address this brand new context.

57. See Angela Dillard and Charles G. Adams, "Chapter 6: The Rev. Albert B. Cleage," *Faith in the City* (Ann Arbor, MI: University of Michigan Press, 2007), 237–279; Susan Williams Smith, *The Book of Jeremiah: The Life and Ministry of Jeremiah A. Wright Jr.* (Cleveland, OH: Pilgrim Press, 2014). In an interview with the author, Wright attributed his African-centered thinking, theology, and worldview to his work as a historian of religions as a student of Charles Long, and his immersion in the works of Cheikh Anta Diop, William Leo Hansberry, Chancellor Williams, John Henrik Clarke, Geneva Smitherman, and John Lovell. The subject of Wright's master's thesis at Howard University under John Lovell was the African-centered perspective of agents and not subjects of their own or European history. In terms of liberation theology, along with Cone, Wright attributes the writings of Gayraud Wilmore and the teachings of Chuck Long, whom Wright studied under at the University of Chicago for six years.

As an example of the move to radicalism and black pride, African American homiletics in the educated strand shifted from the "assumptions that preachers should 'uplift' the congregation through scrupulous grammar, careful elocution, and impressive vocabulary," or as L. Susan Bond says:

> A leadership style that manifested itself in sermons according to what Augustine called the "grand" or "inspirational" style of rhetoric. Sermon illustrations came from Western literary traditions, from Western philosophy, from Western poetry and from sciences. Rhetorical style was marked more by dignity and the kind of "authorities" valued by white homiletical standards.[58]

After the movement to black power the "grand" style gave way to "black English," naturals, dashikis, and Afrocentric thought. This new preaching offered an even more pointed theological critique of white racism and the middle-class values of assimilation and integration. In 1970, Henry H. Mitchell published *Black Preaching*, the landmark text that complimented Cone's *A Black Liberation Theology* and formally introduced the theological academy to black homiletics. Based upon the publishing of *Black Preaching, The Recovery of Preaching* in 1977, and *Celebration and Experience in Preaching* in 1990, Henry H. Mitchell is regarded by many as the "father of African American homiletics."

Another perspective from which to view the emergence of African American preaching in majority consciousness after King is suggested by O. C. Edwards. Edwards notes the invitations that African American clergy received to deliver the Lyman Beecher Lectures at Yale University, historically America's most distinguished majority lectureship in homiletics.[59] The first invitation to an African American clergy was extended to James H. Robinson in 1955, several months before the bus boycott in Montgomery and the prominence of King. Robinson was a Presbyterian minister who focused more on what to preach than how to preach. Robinson did not analyze and discuss the homiletical tradition of the African

---

58. Bond, *Contemporary African American Preaching*, 27.

59. The Lyman Beecher Lectureship was founded in 1871 by a gift from Henry W. Sage of Brooklyn, New York, as a memorial to the great divine whose name it bears, to sponsor an annual series of lectures on a topic appropriate to the work of the ministry. See Edwards, *A History of Preaching*, 710–30.

American church, per se. The fact that Robinson and other later African Americans in the lecture series chose to discuss the commonalities with preaching in general rather than the distinctives of the African American preaching tradition brings up a salient point that would be wise to emphasize here.

There are diverse interests and expertise amongst theoreticians and practitioners of African American preaching such that all African Americans in their presentations do not center on and intend to explain the African American preaching tradition. The preachers who make this choice clearly come out of the African American preaching tradition, and sometimes in their lectures the African American preaching style and genre are clearly evident, but everyone does not feel the need to explicate the explicit differences, but choose to focus on widely shared patterns of commonality across all spectrums of preaching. There is also a strong school of thought in the African American community that does not articulate their preaching as "black." Cleophus J. LaRue clarifies this perspective:

> Those who maintain this view, say there are black preachers who preach, but they don't preach black, they preach the gospel. Chief among the proponents of this position was the late Samuel DeWitt Proctor. . . . Proctor, though not anti-black preaching, simply believed there was too much diversity within the tradition historically or as presently constructed to make accurate generalization. Proctor observed that there African American preaching demonstrated the same diversity as forms of American Christianity and should not be characterized by style of deliver or theological assumptions.[60]

Other leading preachers, such as Gardner Taylor and James Earl Massey, would hold to some form of this perspective. In my view, there is no litmus test of orthodoxy for theoreticians and practitioners of black preaching to label or define themselves as "black preachers." Black preaching is a field and there are many valid points and perspectives, and no one size or shoe of orthodoxy fits all.

---

60. Samuel DeWitt Proctor, pastor emeritus of the Abyssinian Baptist Church in New York and professor of the Martin Luther King Chair in Ethics at Rutgers University. See Cleophus J. LaRue, "Two Ships Passing in the Night," in *What's the Matter with Preaching Today?* ed. Mike Graves (Louisville, KY: Westminster John Knox Press, 2004), 138.

Following in the footsteps of Henry H. Mitchell, I feel the need and call to clarify and articulate the distinctiveness of the African American preaching based upon the need for preservation and contribution of this tradition to the present moment of crisis in Christianity. Other scholars, as they feel called and led in various degrees, choose to follow this same pursuit to clarify the distinctive of African American preaching. I support and applaud the work of every homiletician who works in African American preaching, however they define that work, and even if they do not define their work as African American homiletics.

Here is the list of the distinguished African Americans who gave the Lyman Beecher lectures and the title of their lectures.[61] Many published books have emerged from the lectures and the book publication is listed:

1954–55	James H. Robinson. **"Adventurous Preaching in a World of Change and Trouble."** GreatNeck, NY: Channel Press, 1956.
1973–74	Henry H. Mitchell. **"The Recovery of Preaching."** New York: Harper and Row, 1977.
1975–76	Gardner C. Taylor. **"How Shall They Preach?"** Elgin, IL: Progressive Baptist Publishing House, 1977.
1982–83	Kelly Miller Smith. **"Social Crisis Preaching."** Macon, GA: Mercer University Press, 1984.
1985–86	James A. Forbes. **"The Holy Spirit & Preaching."** Nashville: Abingdon, 1989.
1989–90	Samuel D. Proctor. **"How Shall They Hear: Effective Preaching for Vital Faith."** Valley Forge, PA: Judson Press, 1992.
1992–93	Thomas Hoyt. **"The Church's Preaching in Pluralistic and Ecumenical Contexts."** (not published)

---

61. Source: https://www.library.yale.edu/div/beecher.html

1998	Peter Gomes. **"The Texture of Biblical Preaching: Songs, Letters, and Stories."** (not published)
2004	Otis Moss Jr. **"Preaching as Prophetic Ministry."** (not published)
2008	Renita J. Weems. **"Preaching from the 'Underside' of the Book of Jeremiah: Gods, Goddesses and Matters of Gender."** (not published)
2015	Otis Moss III. **"The Blue Note Gospel: Preaching the Prophetic Blues in a Post Soul World."** Louisville, KY: John Knox Press, 2016.

I have categorized their lectures in the following classifications, which again shows the broad expressions of perspectives and interests in the field of African American homiletics: (1) Spirituality of the Preacher—Taylor and Forbes, (2) Preaching the Biblical Text—Gomes and Weems, (3) Prophetic Preaching—Smith, Proctor, and Moss Jr., (4) Preaching and Contemporary Culture—Robinson, Hoyt, and Moss III, and (5) Distinctiveness of African American preaching—Mitchell. Our next stop will be to discuss the study of the preaching of African American women and womanists.

AFRICAN AMERICAN WOMEN AND WOMANISTS[62]

For most of the history of the African American church, the church subordinated women in clergy ministry roles, forbidding their ordination and refusing to select them as pastors. A convenient divot into which women could be placed was to preach, teach, and lead revivals under the title of "evangelist."[63] Following Teresa L. Fry Brown, of whom we will

---

62. It is important for the reader to note the inclusion of all African American women preachers by the use of the terminology "African American Women and Womanists." Womanism is a significant, yet recent theological and social perspective that some African American women preachers self-identify with. Not all African American women preachers self-identify as womanists.

63. Excellent examples of this subordination abound in *This Is My Story: Testimonies and Sermons of Black Women in Ministry*, ed. Cleophus J. LaRue (Louisville, KY: Westminster John Knox Press, 2005).

say more later, countless women simply "testified" about their experience of God and faith without title and position.[64] Many foremothers of African American preaching—Jarena Lee, Zilpha Elaw, Julia A. Foote, Maria Stewart, Sojourner Truth, and many others—and a myriad of gifted women have labored under, and in spite of, this tragic and exclusionary oppression. Several painful examples hint at the invisibility of African American women preachers by both white and black scholars: (1) the aforementioned Charles V. Hamilton, in his seminal study in 1972, *The Black Preacher in America*, does not mention the tradition of African American female preachers at all; and (2) the preeminent scholar of African American preaching, Henry H. Mitchell, though he uses inclusive language to speak of the preacher, in his two earliest books, *Black Preaching* and *The Recovery of Preaching*, does not include sermons by or address the subject of female preachers.

Despite these restrictions and omissions, many African American women preachers from the 1700s on found creative ways to claim their roles as women, preachers, and religious leaders, and even more directly so in the last forty years. For example, in the twentieth century, one way women preachers subverted restriction was by developing the rhetorical genre of the sermonette-song. In the sermonette-song, preaching, singing, and storytelling are intricately tied together, and "many women carved out preaching and singing circuits without being focused upon as women preachers," such as Willie Mae Ford Smith, Edna Gallmon Cook, Dorothy Norwood, and most famously, Shirley Caesar.[65] Notwithstanding the gains in the last forty years, Cheryl Townsend Gilkes speaks the truth of the challenge of African American women as preachers when she says, "Preaching is the most masculine aspect of black religious rights. Despite the progress of women in ministry, preaching remains overwhelmingly a form of male discourse."[66]

---

64. Also see Anna Florence Carter, *Preaching as Testimony* (Louisville, KY: Westminister John Knox Press, 2007).

65. For more information on the sermonette-song see Simmons and Thomas, *Preaching with Sacred Fire*, 492–97.

66. Cheryl Townsend Gilkes, *If It Wasn't for the Women: Black Women's Experience and Womanist Culture in Church and Community* (Maryknoll, NY: Orbis, 2001), 2001.

Given this virtual invisible reality of African American clergywomen in the church, it would not be surprising to find small amounts of critical attention given to the homiletic theory and methods of African American women. Only in the last forty years has consideration been given to the homiletic of African American women, primarily by African American women themselves. The start of the study of the homiletics of African American women begins in the theological academy, but outside of the field of homiletics.

In 1969, Cheryl J. Sanders published an essay, "The Woman as Preacher," and explored homiletic content as it relates to gender, specifically contrasting the differences between the preaching of African American women and men. Following James Massey's definitions of the four basic sermon forms—expository, narrative, textual, or topical—she studied eighteen sermons by women and eighteen sermons by men. She also surveyed the use of biblical texts, central themes, use of inclusive language, and homiletical task (similar to purpose statement of the sermon) by both. According to Susan Bond, the massive significance of Sanders's work is to

> call into question earlier claims made by male homileticians about theological themes that characterize African American preaching. What may be more accurate is to acknowledge that the world of earlier male African American homileticians is adequate to the task of making generalizations about black male preachers, but does not necessarily reflect the present of particular topics or themes preferred by African American female preachers.[67]

I am sensitive to the fact that I am in the privileged position of an African American male preacher, and the generalizations that I have made to this point concerning African American preaching reflect my social location as Susan Bond suggests. The subject of women preachers and their preaching methods are often left to the end, implying an afterthought after the requisite males have been addressed. This can create the impression that women are inferior or an addendum to the African American preaching tradition. This impression is the furthest reality from

---

67. Bond, *Contemporary African American Preaching*, 142.

my mind and heart, and my goal has been chronological consistency and accuracy. The fact that I directly address the black woman preacher specifically at this point, after having already discussed many male preachers, by no measure implies second-class citizenship. I am simply addressing the point at which the study of the preaching of African American women gained traction in the field of homiletics. While my goal is that African American preaching would be a full partner in the discipline of homiletics, I also unequivocally desire, support, and affirm that African American women be full and equal partners in the traditions of African American preaching. I believe that the homiletics of African American women preachers will continue to both challenge and expand the African American preaching tradition.

Ella Pearson Mitchell, hailed by many as the "Dean of Black Women preachers," was the first to collect the sermons of African American women in a multivolume collection, starting in 1985.[68] Her multivolume collections were an important contribution in preaching circles in that they carved out space for women in the primarily male discourse of preaching, and provided many women who were looking for models access to some of the best preachers in the country. She was a pioneer, a trailblazer, and a preacher-mentor to an entire generation of women preachers, and offered unparalleled support to male preachers, including her husband, Henry H. Mitchell.

Also in 1985, Leontine T. C. Kelly published an essay on preaching in the black tradition. She critiques the African American church, consistent with all churches, as being sexist, and highlights that the strictest form of gender bias resides in preaching. Kelly's approach was more outspoken in regard to the domination of women clergy by male patriarchy than Mitchell, but not as critical as some of the next generation of women scholars and the emergence of the religious and social change theory of womanism.[69]

---

68. Ella Pearson Mitchell, *Those Preaching Women*, 3 vols. (Valley Forge, PA: Judson Press, 1985) and *Women: To Preach or Not to Preach? 21 Outstanding Black Preachers Say Yes* (Valley Forge, PA: Judson Press, 1991).

69. Leontine T. C. Kelly, "Preaching in the Black Tradition," in *Women Ministers*, ed. Judith L. Weidman (San Francisco: Harper & Row, 1985), 67–76.

The term *womanism* was first coined by author Alice Walker in *In Search of Our Mother's Gardens: Womanist Prose*.[70] She explains that the term *womanist* is derived from the Southern folk expression of mothers to female children, "acting womanish," or like a woman. The womanish girl exhibits willful, courageous, and outrageous behavior that is considered to be beyond the scope of established societal norms. The womanish child is acting grown-up or interested in grown-up doings. The term is a metaphor for black women being responsible, in charge, serious—fully grown. At its core, womanism addresses the realities and everyday concerns, issues, and experiences of black women. Womanism issues a distinct challenge for inclusion to dominant male and female white theological approaches, as well as black theology and African American male scholars, homiletical and otherwise.

Key figures in womanism have been Jacqueline Grant, Katie G. Cannon, and Delores Williams. Of the three, Cannon writes more directly on the preaching of black women. Though not a homiletician in the strictest terms, she lectures, preaches, and wrote an important article connecting womanism and black preaching, "Womanist Interpretation and Preaching in the Black Church."[71] The groundbreaking nature of her article is highlighted by her insight that heretofore, black preaching had not asked questions about womanist interpretation and womanist theological studies had not included preaching. She argues that this connection is critically important because the majority of adherents of black preaching are women.

Womanist interpretation of preaching challenges conventional interpretations of women as "sin-bringing Eve," or "prostituting Mary Magdalene" and the like, in other words, any sexist-racist social, political, theological, or ethical construct that gives women a zero image of themselves. Using the feminist liberation interpretation method of Schussler Fiorenza, Cannon is able to "identify and critique sermonic texts that express and

---

70. Alice Walker, *In Search of Our Mothers' Gardens: Womanist Prose* (San Diego: Harcourt Brace Jovanich, 1983).

71. Katie G. Cannon, "Womanist Interpretation and Preaching in the Black Church," in *Katie's Canon: Womanism and the Soul of the Black Community* (New York: Continuum, 1995), 113–21.

maintain patriarchal historical conditioning" and "reproduce and shape the liberative reality for all members of the worshipping community."[72] In terms of homiletical method of the structuring and delivery of sermon, Cannon subscribes to the homiletical method of Isaac R. Clark, her homiletics professor in seminary. Cannon sums up her methodology in this way:

> Using Clark's tools and methods on preaching in the Black church and relating them to Schussler Fiorenza's most recent writings on feminist liberationist criticism, we can provide precise answers to the questions of (1) how meaning is constructed, (2) whose interests are served, and (3) what kind of worlds are envisioned in Black sacred rhetoric. [73]

Cannon's second major contribution to African American homiletics is her formal presentation of the homiletical method of Isaac Rufus Clark.[74] Cannon was chosen by Clark to "make sure that his distinct homiletical method received the critical attention it deserves in the twenty-first century."[75] Clark's distinct method can be summed up in this non-negotiable theological mandate: "To apply the principles of rhetoric to the particular ends and means of the Christian gospel, for the purpose of liberation, reconciliation, and maturation in the deepest theological sense of the term, so that professionals of the Word of God will never be guilty of unconsciously tampering with people's souls."[76]

Clark also supplies a definition of black preaching from the antebellum era to the present that I return to again and again in my teaching, writing, and preaching. It is the most fruitful definition of black preaching that I have ever heard: *Preaching is divine activity, wherein the word of God*

---

72. Ibid., 115.

73. Ibid., 121.

74. Katie Geneva Cannon, *Teaching Preaching: Isaac Rufus Clark and Black Sacred Rhetoric* (New York: Continuum, 2007).

75. Ibid., 15.

76. Ibid., 23.

is proclaimed or announced on a contemporary issue with an ultimate response to our God.[77]

Bettye Collier Thomas, a scholar of African American women's history, made a vast and significant contribution to the study of the preaching of African American women with the publishing of her *Daughters of Thunder*, an anthology of nineteenth- and twentieth-century sermons. *Daughters of Thunder* clearly demonstrates the ability of African American women to shape effective and powerful sermons to "proclaim the Word of God on a contemporary issue with an ultimate response to God."[78] Sermons by black women were rarely collected or recorded, making this anthology an invaluable resource not only for scholars, but also for women who are looking for historical role models, and men who have an interest in studying good preaching.

Teresa Fry Brown's vast and valuable contribution to African American homiletics and the preaching of African American women speaks to the unappreciated and devalued gifts of African American women to the church. She argues that though women have been restricted in the pulpit, they have spoken clearly in families, communities, and churches. Fry Brown sketches out a framework for a womanist homiletic in her 1998 chapter "Renovating Sorrow's Kitchen," in *Preaching Justice: Ethnic and Cultural Perspectives*.[79] In *God Don't Like Ugly*, she explores the moral discourse of mothers, grandmothers, sisters, aunts, play cousins, and other women through the oral tradition.[80] This impartation of spiritual values happens through music, prayer, literature, and folk tales. She lifts and brings to consciousness this important moral discourse and makes it plain that the African American community talks about God more than just from the pulpit.

---

77. Ibid., 18.

78. Bettye Collier-Thomas, *Daughters of Thunder: Black Women Preachers and Their Sermons, 1850–1979* (San Francisco, CA: Jossey-Bass, 1998).

79. Teresa Fry Brown, "An African American Woman's Perspective: Renovating Sorrow's Kitchen," in *Preaching Justice: Ethnic and Cultural Perspectives*, ed. Christine M. Smith (Cleveland, OH: United Church Press, 1998).

80. Teresa L. Fry Brown, *God Don't Like Ugly: African American Women Handing on Spiritual Values* (Nashville: Abingdon Press, 2000).

She follows this discussion of the moral discourse of women with *Weary Throats and New Songs: Black Women Proclaiming God's Word*. This book provides an invaluable and brief review of the rich history of black female proclaimers by analyzing the particularities of contemporary black women preachers' call experiences, models and mentors, sermon preparation, content, delivery, and personhood. She argues the term *preachers* for black women is delimiting because there are "thousands of African American women who 'Say a Word' for God, but are not ordained or operate under a different rubric."[81] She calls them "proclaimers," and therefore calls black women's preaching discourse proclamation. Based on surveys of black women in forty-one states and thirty denominations, she provides a means of assessment of the distinctive nature of the black women's proclamation, that is, "living testimonies, songs about what black women actually do in the preaching moment rather than what is theoretically assumed."[82]

Elaine Flake crafts a womanist praxis of preaching that offers a healing hermeneutic of scripture to black women wounded by virtue of their gender and race.[83] Calling all preachers of every race and gender into accountability, Flake offers a concrete womanist paradigm that both offers practical application to the perspectives and theories of womanism and calls male and female preachers to offer liberation and empowerment to marginalized and hurting African American women. Flake closes her book with several sermons that demonstrate her hermeneutic of healing.

Donna E. Allen published *Toward a Womanist Homiletic: Katie Cannon, Alice Walker and Emancipatory Proclamation*, and moves to fully establish a womanist homiletic. Allen believes that a womanist homiletic[84] contributes significantly to the understanding of black preaching by both challenging and expanding the African American preaching tradition. She

---

81. Teresa L. Fry Brown, *Weary Throats and New Songs: Black Women Proclaiming God's Word* (Nashville: Abingdon Press, 2003).

82. Ibid., 17.

83. M. Elaine Collins Flake (author) and Kathryn V. Stanley (editor), *God in Her Midst: Preaching Healing to Wounded Women* (Valley Forge, PA: Judson Press, 2007).

84. Donna E. Allen, *Toward a Womanist Homiletic: Katie Cannon, Alice Walker and Emancipatory Proclamation* (New York: Peter Lang Publishing, 2013).

utilizes Alice Walker's definition of womanism, Katie Cannon's womanist critique of black preaching, and Aristotle's rhetorical categories of ethos, logos, and pathos to foster an "emancipatory praxis" in the world. Allen argues that Cannon's womanist critique emphasizes the linguistic elements of the logos of black preaching and considers this both a contribution and a limitation. Because womanist preaching is "trans-rational," that is, "an act of embodiment and performed identity," and therefore significantly more than a rational mode of communication, Allen contends that it is necessary for purposes of critical analysis and insight to extend logos to include Aristotle's final two means of persuasion, ethos and pathos. [85]

Allen argues that to fully engage the preaching of womanists, one must engage rhetorical criticism. Following Sonja K. Foss, Allen defines rhetorical criticism as the ability to understand the various options available to speakers in the construction of messages, and how they work together to create effects in the message. Rhetorical criticism is vital because it allows listeners to ascertain, and potentially question, the rhetorical choices made in the construction of sermons because listeners can see rhetorical possibilities other than those selected by the speaker. This ability to perceive other possibilities and question the speaker's choices is the heart of rhetorical criticism, and womanist homiletic would make this skill available to congregations as necessary to help the congregation and preacher move to an emancipatory praxis. Listeners would be equipped with a model that allows them to critically engage the sermon. To model and apply this theory of rhetorical criticism and its ability to move the hearer to emancipatory praxis, Allen applies rhetorical criticism to the womanist preaching of the Prathia Hall. By her insightful analysis of Hall, Allen clarifies how womanist homiletic both challenges and expands the black preaching tradition.

Allen's work is a major contribution to the black preaching tradition by challenging the rhetorical dominance of the African American male by clarifying the emancipatory praxes of womanist preaching, and opening of new windows of analysis of black preaching, such as the inclusion of rhetorical criticism as part of homiletical inquiry. I will follow her lead and

---

85. Ibid., 6.

inject the method of rhetorical criticism into my own analysis of black preaching in the next chapter.

Martha Simmons makes a significant contribution to black preaching in *Preaching with Sacred Fire: An Anthology of African American Preaching, from 1750 to the Present.* Aside from the momentous impact of the first anthology of African American preaching with groundbreaking research and inclusion of women as full partners into the canon of African American preaching alongside African American men, the book features an important article: "Whooping: The Musicality of African Americans Past and Present."[86] Simmons has provided a significant contribution to the African American preaching tradition in the overall work of the anthology, and also with the study of an almost underexamined and influential aspect of African American preaching, whooping.

One final important point: just as a plethora of conferences and institutes exist in the African American preaching tradition with primarily male preaching as a focus, a significant number of forums, conferences, and service formats have arisen to celebrate and explore the preaching of black women, such as all-female Seven Last Word services, Woman Preach! Inc., Women in Ministry Conference, and the Ella Mitchell Preaching Conference.[87] African American women are forming conferences and assemblages to support, encourage, advocate, critique, and define the homiletical methods of African American women.

Debra J. Mumford, in *Exploring Prosperity Preaching: Biblical Health, Wealth, and Wisdom,* does not discuss the distinctiveness of the preaching of African American women per se, but analyzes the seeds of prosperity preaching in the black church.[88] She explores the following: What are the seeds of truth in prosperity preaching? Why does it have such an appeal in today's African American church? She traces the roots of prosperity

---

86. Simmons and Thomas, *Preaching with Sacred Fire,* 864–84.

87. For WomenPreach! Inc., http://womanpreach.org; for Women in Ministry Conference, www.cynthialhaleministries.org/index.php?option=com_content&view=article&id=9&Itemid=18; for the Ella Mitchell Preaching Conference, http://wilinternationalllc.vpweb.com/ella-mitchell-conference-2.

88. Debra J. Mumford, *Exploring Prosperity Preaching: Biblical Health, Wealth, and Wisdom* (Valley Forge, PA: Judson Press, 2012).

preaching to its Word of Faith origins and examines its common teachings, carefully weighing biblical proof texts against the larger scriptural testimony concerning our health, wealth, and spiritual wisdom. Not all African American women homileticians are solely focused on the distinctiveness of preaching of black women, but, as we suggested with African American male preachers, they do address critical issues in the culture and community, as well as the commonalities of the preaching of African American women with all other preaching traditions.

In summation of all the presented material in this chapter, I would like to establish taxonomy of the academic study of African American preaching.

Taxonomy of the Study of African American Preaching

Admittedly, taxonomy is at best an artificial pedagogical construct to survey and organize in broad strokes a large body of literature, in this case, the homiletical and historical emergence of African American preaching. The first thing to note is that this taxonomy is primarily concerned with published works on the methodological analysis of African American preaching. A fuller taxonomy would require an extensive investigation of other sources, such as previously unpublished material as well as material preserved in electronic form, in oral tradition, and in other media.

Secondly, the taxonomy is principally concerned with major books and a few key articles because to include all of the articles and the total number of books would make this discussion cumbersome and unwieldy. For example, singular collections of sermons are not listed herein. The major concern is methodological analysis as much as possible.

Thirdly, though an author might have multiple publications, and therefore could be listed in several eras, my focus is on a writer's first book, when the author initially entered the published discussion of the field. Other major works by authors will be listed in the full bibliography at the end of the book.

Fourthly, the typology includes scholars both outside and inside the field of homiletics, as well as pastors, and activists, who found the need to write on the method and theory of African American homiletics and whose work is significant for understanding the unfolding of the field.

Next, the attempt is made to follow a strictly chronological order of publication, which means that some works fit very loosely within the assigned headings, especially works that appeared in the same time frames as or close to the dividing lines of the taxonomy.

In summary, my purpose in the creation of this limited and artificial typology is to allow a framework for discussion such that various scholars can discuss perspectives and concerns that strengthen research and analysis because typologies give some level of organization and coherence as well as historical accounting to a field.

The historical development of the study of African American preaching has four eras: the First Era B.K. (1750–1968) (Before King), the Second Era A.K. (1969–1995) (After King), the Third Era (1996–2014), and the Fourth Era (2015–). Underneath each era, I will list important books that helped to shape the direction of the era.

The First Era B.K. (1750–1968)—African American preachers, alongside the development of the African American church, utilized the oral and religious traditions of West Africa and the brutal chattel slave and racist experience of America to shape a principally Christian theological and rhetorical, as well as folk and intellectual, tradition of African American preaching. The First Era is the formation of the beginnings of African American preaching as a formal discipline of study. The study and inquiry of the discipline starts principally outside of the theological academy in the oral tradition and the interdisciplinary fields of folklore, history, social science, public address, rhetoric, English, and others. Based upon the "homiletical epiphany" of the majority of American society to the power of African American preaching to move people and change society during the civil rights movement, interest in African American preaching began to soar in American culture and homiletical community. As a result of the surge of interest in African American preaching, the end of the First Era can be demarcated as the death of Martin Luther King Jr. in 1968. Here are several of the principal works of the First Era:

W. E. B. Dubois, *The Souls of Black Folk* (1903)

Carter G. Woodson, *The History of the Negro Church* (1921)

James Weldon Johnson, *God's Trombones* (1927)

Benjamin Elijah Mays and Joseph William Nicholson, *The Negro's Church* (1933)

William H. Pipes, *Say Amen, Brother: A Study in American Frustration* (1951)

James H. Robinson, *Adventuresome Preaching* (1956)

The Second Era A.K. (1969–1995)—In the aftermath of the death of King, the first works in African American homiletics in the theological/homiletical academic community emerge, principally written by African American males. The principles that characterize the Second Era of the development of the discipline of black preaching are individuation and homiletical hermeneutics.

Individuation is the natural process in biological and human community when a cell, person, or group, as an expression of their own identity, separate from their parents, originating body, context, or field. Black preaching self-consciously finds its own voice and shapes its own identity by individuating from and contrasting itself with principally Euro-centric homiletical perspectives. This is the first step in African American scholarship shaping its own interpretation of its homiletics, which is designated as homiletical hermeneutics.

As we have mentioned already, there is diversity in the African American preaching tradition and some individuate in more contrasting and definitive terms, explicating the distinctiveness of black preaching as their hermeneutical lens, such as Henry H. Mitchell, Lawrence L. Beale, Mervyn Warren, Evans E. Crawford Jr., William B. McClain, Olin P. Moyd, and Warren Stewart.

For others, black preaching is the conversation partner through which parallels are made to the commonalities of black preaching with the broader homiletical community, such as the spirituality of the preacher found in the work of James Earl Massey, J. Alfred Smith, Gardner C. Taylor, and James A. Forbes. The homiletical hermeneutics of black women and womanists emerge as black women and womanists individuate and offer a prophetic critique of the exclusionary practices of particularly African American and Euro-centric males. African American women and womanists articulate their own preaching models and methods, inclusive of Cheryl J. Sanders, Ella Pearson Mitchell, Leontine T. C. Kelly, and Katie G. Canon. James H. Harris, Samuel D. Proctor, and Kelly Miller Smith articulate liberation and prophetic preaching as their hermeneutic for black preaching. The interdisciplinary nature of the study of black preaching continues in the work of Bruce R. Rosenberg, Gerald L. Davis, Jeff Todd Titon, Keith D. Miller, Charles V. Hamilton, and Jon Michael Spencer. The following works principally shape the Second Era:

Cheryl J. Sanders, "The Woman as Preacher" (1969)

Henry H. Mitchell, *Black Preaching* (1970)

Bruce A. Rosenberg, *Can These Bones Live? The Art of the African American Folk Preacher* (1970)

Charles V. Hamilton, *The Black Preacher in America* (1972)

James Earl Massey, *The Responsible Pulpit* (1974)

Lawrence L. Beale, *Towards a Black Homiletic* (1977)

Gardner C. Taylor, *How Shall They Preach* (1977)

Mervyn Warren, *Black Preaching: Truth and Soul* (1977)

J. Alfred Smith, *Preach On!* (1984)

Kelly Miller Smith, *Social Crisis Preaching* (1984)

Warren Stewart, *Interpreting God's Word in Black Preaching* (1984)

Gerald L. Davis, *I Got the Word in Me and I Can Sing It, You Know: A Study of the Performed African American Sermon* (1985). (Like Rosenberg)

Leontine T. C. Kelly, "Preaching in the Black Tradition" (1985)

Ella Pearson Mitchell, *Those Preaching Women*, 3 vols. (1985)

Jon Michael Spencer, *Sacred Symphony: The Chanted Sermon of the Black Preacher* (1987)

Samuel D. Proctor, *Preaching about Crisis in the Community* (1988)

James A. Forbes, *The Holy Spirit and Preaching* (1989)

Jeff Todd Titon, *Give Me This Mountain: Life, History, and Selected Sermons of C. L. Franklin* (1989)

James Earl Massey, *Designing the Sermon: Order and Movement in Preaching* (1989)

Keith D. Miller, *Voice of Deliverance: The Language of Martin Luther King Jr. and Its Sources* (1992)

Evans E. Crawford Jr., *The Hum: Call and Response in African American Preaching* (1995)

William B. McClain, *Come Sunday: The Liturgy of Zion* (1990)

Katie G. Canon, "Womanist Interpretation and Preaching in the Black Church" (1995)

James H. Harris, *Preaching Liberation* (1995)

Olin P. Moyd, *The Sacred Art: Preaching and Theology in the African American Tradition* (1995)

The Third Era (1996–2014)—The process of individuation and homiletical hermeneutics continue and new works of scholarship move the field in new directions. There is critical attention to methodological explanation and documentation of black preaching, such as the scholarship of Richard Lischer, Susan L. Bond, and myself. Cleophus J. LaRue fully explicates the unique theological dimensions of black preaching as the most appropriate hermeneutical lens to view black preaching. Dale P. Andrews develops deep connections between the field of practical theology, black theology, and folk religion. Both Andrews and Katie Cannon begin discussion of understandings of pedagogy to form teachers and black preachers in the work of preaching. Kenyatta Gilbert also utilizes the hermeneutical lens of practical theology to explicate the importance of trivocal nature of black preaching, as prophet, priest, and sage. Robert Smith utilizes black preaching as a conversation partner to illustrate doctrinal preaching that "dances." Martha Simmons edits essays on the future of preaching in honor of Henry H. Mitchell. The clarification of the preaching of black women and womanists continue in the work of Betty Collier-Thomas, Teresa Fry Brown, Elaine Flake, and Donna E. Allen. Luke Powery continues the work in the hermeneutics of pneumatology and spirituality of the preacher. Gennifer Brooks continues to work in the hermeneutics of the commonality of black preaching with the broader homiletical community. Noted black preacher E. K. Bailey and white preacher Warren W. Wiersbe discuss the dynamics of pulpit ministry and what each can learn from the other's tradition and different perspectives. The hermeneutics of preaching and contemporary culture are explored in the work of Stephanie Y. Mitchem, Debra J. Mumford, and Marvin McMickle. Adam L. Bond utilizes the hermeneutic of black public to discuss the preaching of Samuel DeWitt Proctor. The following works shape and direct this Third Era:

Martha J. Simmons, ed. *Preaching on the Brink: The Future of Homiletics* (1996)

Richard Lischer, *The Preacher King* (1997)

Frank A. Thomas, *They Like to Never Quit Praisin' God: The Role of Celebration in Preaching* (1997)

CHAPTER ONE

Bettye Collier-Thomas, *Daughters of Thunder: Black Women Preachers and Their Sermons, 1850–1979* (1998)

Cleophus J. LaRue, *The Heart of Black Preaching* (1999)

Marvin E. McMickle, *Preaching to the Black Middle Class* (2000)

Valentino Lassiter, *Martin Luther King in the African American Preaching Tradition* (2001)

Dale P. Andrews, *Practical Theology for Black Churches: Bridging Black Theology and African American Folk Religion* (2002)

Susan L. Bond, *Contemporary African American Preaching: Diversity in Theory and Style* (2003)

Teresa L. Fry Brown, *Weary Throats and New Songs: Black Women Proclaiming* (2003)

E. K. Bailey and Warren W. Wiersbe, *Preaching in Black & White: What We Can Learn from Each Other* (2003)

Kirk Byron Jones, *The Jazz of Preaching* (2004)

Gerald Lamont Thomas, *African American Preaching: The Contribution of Dr. Gardner C. Taylor* (2004)

Katie Geneva Cannon, *Teaching Preaching: Isaac Rufus Clark and Black Sacred Rhetoric* (2007).

M. Elaine Collins Flake (author) and Kathryn V. Stanley (editor), *God in Her Midst: Preaching Healing to Wounded Women* (2007).

Stephanie Y. Mitchem, *Name It or Claim It? Prosperity Preaching in the Black Church* (2007)

Robert Smith Jr., *Doctrine That Dances: Bringing Doctrinal Preaching and Teaching to Life* (2008)

William Clair Turner Jr., *Preaching That Makes the Word Plain: Doing Theology in the Crucible of Life* (2008)

Luke A. Powery, *Spirit Speech: Lament and Celebration in Preaching* (2009)

Gennifer Brooks, *Good News Preaching: Offering the Gospel in Every Sermon* (2009)

Timothy George, James Earl Massey, and Robert Smith Jr., eds. *Our Sufficiency Is of God: Essays on Preaching in Honor of Gardner C. Taylor* (2010)

Martha Simmons and Frank A. Thomas eds., *Preaching with Sacred Fire: An Anthology of African American Preaching, 1750 to the Present* (2010)

Gregory Howard, *Black Sacred Rhetoric* (2010)

Kenyatta Gilbert, *The Journey and Promise of African American Preaching* (2011)

Debra J. Mumford, *Exploring Prosperity Preaching: Biblical Health, Wealth, and Wisdom* (2012)

Donna E. Allen, *Toward a Womanist Homiletic: Katie Cannon, Alice Walker and Emancipatory Proclamation* (2013)

Adam L. Bond, *The Imposing Preacher: Samuel DeWitt Proctor and Black Public Faith* (2013)

Lerone A. Martin, *Preaching on Wax: The Phonograph and the Shaping of Modern African American Religion* (2014)

Peter M. Wherry, *Preaching Funerals in the Black Church: Bringing Perspective to Pain* (2014)

The Fourth Generation (2015–)—Admittedly, the choice of this date of 2015 for the start of the fourth era is fairly arbitrary. All historians say that the present history is the hardest history about which to write, but historians/scholars are called to make the best judgments they can, recognizing that all scholarship about the present and the future is limited. Therefore, everything that I am about to write about this Fourth Era is "seeing in a glass darkly." The future, in the wisdom of God, may give birth to forms of homiletic expression that are as of yet unnoticed and unborn.

Books published in this era will expand the study of the African American preaching tradition by insights on the hermeneutical and homiletical connections between African American preaching and discourses of other marginalized communities, such as Asian Americans, Latin@, Koreans, as well as the global expansion of the study of black preaching into the homiletics of the African Diaspora, the Global South, and marginalized communities around the world.[89] Cleophus J. LaRue will soon publish *Colored Preaching: The Shape of Christian Proclamation in the Global South*. Women and womanist homileticians will carve new insights into black preaching through scholarship on the hermeneutics of the preaching experience of black women. Several young scholars have expressed interest in the hermeneutics and homiletics of black preaching encompassing the task of pulpit preaching both inside and outside the Christian church, what was coined by a group of young scholars as "communicative expression." They meant that African American homiletics would also study music, poetry, public discourse, new media, hip-hop, and other sacred and secular cultural forms of expression. Jared Alcantara uses the term "crossover preaching" as a hermeneutical lens to study the preaching of Gardner C. Taylor. Otis Moss III focuses on the blues as a hermeneutical lens to study black preaching.

Jared E. Alcantara, *Crossover Preaching: Intercultural-Improvisational Homiletics in Conversation with Gardner C. Taylor* (2015)

Otis Moss III, *Blue Note Preaching in a Post-Soul World: Finding Hope in an Age of Despair* (2015)

---

89. Examples of global homiletical work of marginalized communities are Dalit homiletics professor Alfred Stephen's book *Homiletics from the Underside: The Art of Contextual Preaching* (Madurai, India: ECHO, 2014), Sarah Travis's book *Decolonizing Preaching: The Pulpit as Postcolonial Space* (Eugene, OR: Cascade Books, 2014), and Pablo A. Jimenez, "If You Just Close Your Eyes: Postcolonial Perspectives in Preaching from the Carribean," www.drpablojimenez.com/adobe/Homiletic_PJ_Postcolonial.pdf.

Chapter Two
NEGRO EXPRESSION, SIGNIFYING, AND THE RHETORIC OF AFRICAN AMERICAN PREACHING

African American preaching is fundamentally both a rhetorical and theological enterprise. African American preachers utilized the oral traditions of West Africa and the slave experience of America to shape verbal and nonverbal expressions (sounds and gestures) that were inherently and necessarily rhetorical and theological. Within the African American preaching tradition, there has not been a hard and fast debate distinguishing rhetoric and theology, that is, a total separation of the art of persuasion from theological reasoning in the preaching process. In contradistinction, in the history of Western preaching, there has been an ongoing discussion of whether or not preaching is a theological or rhetorical act. There have been times, such as the first four centuries of the Christian era, when the church was clear that the word of God did not need rhetorical processes to express its truth, and other times, such as the late twentieth century, when David Buttrick and the New Homiletic declared rhetorical frames of reference as substantive and necessary for a new hearing of the gospel.

In this chapter, I will briefly trace the long and circuitous relationship between theology and rhetoric in Western preaching. I will argue that in the contemporary field of homiletics, there are scholars such as John McClure, Fred B. Craddock, James F. Kay, Lucy Lind Hogan, Robert Reid, and André Resner Jr. who articulate the valuable role of rhetoric in the preaching process, but on the whole, rhetorical methods of persuasion are accessed at the close of the sermon preparation process after firmly establishing that the sermon is a reasoned argument. As a brief example, Fred B. Craddock states in his classic work *Preaching*, "The principle of procedure fundamental to the task of sermon preparation is this: the process of arriving at something to say is to be distinguished from the process of determining how to say it. This statement should be printed in placard-size letters suitable for cutting out and fastening across the top of the minister's desk."[1]

Then, I will add the voice of African American preaching to the discussion by exploring rhetorical processes in African American preaching. The oral traditions of West Africa and the brutal experience of slavery helped to shape what Zora Neale Hurston calls "Negro expression" and what Henry Louis Gates, the master trope of black rhetoric, calls "signifying." It is this unique construction of meaning through Negro expression and signifying that inherently joins the theological and rhetorical in African American preaching. I want to begin with a discussion of the historical relationship between homiletics and rhetoric in the Western preaching tradition.

THE HISTORICAL RELATIONSHIP BETWEEN HOMILETICS AND RHETORIC

Fred B. Craddock opens his article "Is There Still Room for Rhetoric?" by asking whether the marriage between homiletics and rhetoric should be terminated.[2] He comments that the marriage has been such a long one that respect for history demands that there be no divorce without careful reflection. In the spirit of careful reflection, I would like to offer a brief recounting of the relationship between rhetoric and homiletics.

Lucy Lind Hogan and Robert Reid point out that the preaching of the New Testament had its roots in the preaching of the synagogue, of which

---

1. Fred B. Craddock, *Preaching* (Nashville: Abingdon, 1985), 84.

2. Fred B. Craddock, "Is There Still Room for Rhetoric?" in *Preaching on the Brink: The Future of Homiletics*, ed. Martha J. Simmons (Nashville: Abingdon, 1996), 66–74.

Luke 14:4 and Acts 13:16-41 are models.[3] Jewish worship began with a reading from Torah or the Prophets. Then, a rabbi or invited guest offered an interpretive lecture that applied the interpretation to the life of the congregation. While this was the case inside the Jewish community, much earlier Christian preaching was offered to non-Jewish and Greco-Roman audiences who were trained by the educational system in "eloquence," or rhetoric. Students in antiquity "were literally drilled on ways to make 'plausible' arguments and techniques to 'embroider and stylize' phrases if the occasion called for it."[4] Works by Aristotle, Cicero, and Quintilian were commonplace as handbooks on eloquence.

As Christianity moved outside of its Jewish roots and increasingly became crosscultural, rhetoric was considered the basic primer in effective communication for citizens of the Roman Empire and the skill of oratory was mandatory preparation for entry into civic life.[5] Craddock suggests that the use of rhetoric in communicating the gospel as a practice is at least as old as the New Testament itself:

> [The New Testament] employs many rhetorical strategies: alliteration, repletion, inclusion, refrain, contrast, double negatives, multiple nouns without conjunctions, use of nouns as adjectives, and others. In fact, rhetoric so dominated the curricula of academics in the ancient Mediterranean world that it was almost impossible for public communication, oral and written, to be free of it.[6]

During the next four centuries of the Christian era, the form of Jewish preaching that began in the New Testament evolved to what became known as the "homily" and principally functioned as a talk or a formal conversation to interpret and apply the gospel for either the converted or unconverted. It was in this period that the early church began to reject the formal art of rhetoric in preaching based upon the argument that rhetoric was concerned not with truth, but with whether the speech would appeal

---

3. Lucy Lind Hogan and Robert Reid, *Connecting with the Congregation: Rhetoric and the Art of Preaching* (Nashville: Abingdon, 1999), 27.

4. Ibid., 27.

5. Ibid., 28.

6. Craddock, "Is There Still Room for Rhetoric?," 16.

to the crowds. Aristotle taught that rhetorical argument is different from logical or dialectical argument. Logical argument emulated the certainty of mathematics in its quest for truth. Dialectical argument uses arguments that are supposed to be "valid" to reason its way to truths most educated people would be willing to accept. In rhetorical arguments, what matters is not truth, but whether arguments appear persuasive to the crowds. Rhetoric fell into disfavor because from the Christian perspective, "Christian scripture was treated as the final, authoritative *truth*, and it was the Spirit that bore witness to the *truth* of God's word, not the opinion of persuaded audience members . . . the artifice of persuasive techniques would only obfuscate the *truth* and deny the work of the Spirit."[7]

Augustine, the African theologian, faced this polarized situation between rhetoric and preaching, and provided the first "textbook" in homiletics, *On Christian Doctrine*. Augustine, in this famous work, reclaimed the connection between rhetorical principles and preaching: "There are also certain rules for a more copious kind of argument, which is called *eloquence*, and these rules are not the less true that they can be used for persuading men of what is false; but as they can be used to enforce the truth as well, it is not the faculty itself that is to be blamed."[8]

Augustine himself was a teacher of rhetoric before he became a Christian, and his adaptation of rhetoric to the study and practice of homiletics dominated preaching well into the twentieth century. Augustine added intentional rhetorical skills of persuasion to the tradition of the homily with a focus on confronting the false teaching of heretics.

In the eleventh century, a significant change occurred as preaching moved from the homily form to scripture examined "not as text, but *for* a text which the preaching might thematically amplify."[9] Rhetoric and preaching were cautiously connected with the publication of Alain de Lille's *On Preacher's Art* (ca. 1199), the first homiletic textbook composed as a rhetoric of preaching. There was an explosion of rhetorics of preach-

---

7. Hogan and Reid, *Connecting with the Congregation: Rhetoric and the Art of Preaching*, 34.

8. Augustine, *On Christian Doctrine*, 2.40 and 4.17.

9. Hogan and Reid, *Connecting with the Congregation: Rhetoric and the Art of Preaching*, 36.

ing, eventually leading to Robert of Basevorn, in his fourteenth-century *Form of Preaching* (ca. 1322), describing an extensive structure for a "three point" sermon that develops a theme. Sermons became a tightly reasoned argument, which was highly suited for the doctrinal program of the Reformation. O. Wesley Allen argues that the Franciscans and Dominicans developed a similar form of preaching called the "university sermon":

> The approach is to take a central theme and break it into three points, each of which is then divided into three subsections. The university sermon was the beginning of the three-point, two joke, and one poem sermon. The approach is propositional: name the point or thesis at the beginning and break it into smaller didactic propositions for analysis.[10]

In contrast to the university sermon, Allen also identifies the "Puritan Plain" style of preaching. Arising from Calvinism in England and New England, the form de-emphasized less thematic preaching of three points and more exposition of scripture:

> There are three major parts of the sermon—first, commentary on the ancient text in its ancient setting; second, eternal doctrinal points drawn from the exposition of the ancient text; and third, application of the doctrine to the current lives of those in the congregation—biblical exegesis, theological interpretation, and moral exhortation.[11]

Allen indicates that both of these forms are deductive in logic and propositional in structure and together dominated preaching in the West for four or five centuries. Preaching had become synonymous with rational argument and the Puritans picked up these forms of sermon as rational argument.

James F. Kay suggests that Euro-American homiletics began when John Witherspoon (1723–1794) placed "the New Rhetoric" of the Scottish Enlightenment at the center of Princeton College. Published posthumously in 1808, Witherspoon's "Lectures on Eloquence" was the first American rhetorical treatise and reflected on the practice of preaching in

---

10. O. Wesley Allen, Jr., *The Renewed Homiletic* (Minneapolis: Fortress Press, 2010), 3.
11. Ibid., 3.

CHAPTER TWO

light of rhetorical theory. The main proponents of the New Rhetoric were Witherspoon, George Campbell (1719–1796), and Hugh Blair (1718–1800), and for these rhetoricians, according to Kay, "Homiletics, therefore, is a 'species' of rhetoric, eloquence adapted for use in the pulpit."[12]

Kay then traces this rhetoric of preaching thread from Witherspoon to John A. Broadus:

> Beginning with Witherspoon, homiletics in America has generally operated within a rhetorical, rather than a theological, frame of reference.... John A. Broadus (1827–1895) decisively defined homiletics for theological education when he wrote in 1870 that "homiletics may be a branch of rhetoric, or a kindred art, or we must regard homiletics as rhetorical applied to this particular kind of speaking," that is, preaching.[13]

In Broadus's *On Preparation and Delivery of Sermons*, first published in 1870, homiletics is dependent on the rhetorical categories of argument theory and logical proof. Allen summarizes Broadus: "According to this text, a sermon should have a guiding subject that is named in the opening, often in the title itself. This subject should be argued persuasively, illustrated to make the abstract concrete and understandable, and applied so that the truth unpacked is given explicit relevance for life."[14] Broadus brought Protestant homiletics into the full embrace of Enlightenment rationalism.

Despite the commitment of the New Rhetoric to rhetorical preaching, doubts strongly surfaced about preaching as eloquence, eloquence without sufficient attention to theological and ethical content and implication. George Campbell admits that the eloquence of the Crusades too easily stirred up hatred and intolerance, and the positive role of eloquence in motivating us toward goodness is almost impossible. One generation later, John Quincy Adams (1767–1848) confessed that classical rhetoric, when it comes to the pulpit, "entirely fails us." Kay says, "Though not a professional theologian, this Harvard rhetorician and future President of

---

12. James F. Kay, "Reorientation: Homiletics as Theologically Authorized Rhetoric," *Princeton Seminary Bulletin* 24, no. 1 (2003): 17.

13. Ibid., 18.

14. Allen, *The Renewed Homiletic*, 4.

the United States, perceives that something new enters history with the advent of Christian preaching; something that makes it so unlike other forms of public address that rhetoric proves unreliable as the frame of reference."[15]

Karl Barth (1886–1968) fully articulates what is the primary difference in Christian preaching that makes rhetoric totally unnecessary: the sermon is nothing other than the word of God.

Barth believes that rhetoric cannot package the word of God. It simply is not possible for the preacher in his or her own power or the power of eloquence to make the preacher's words become God's word. God must make the speech the word of God and not rhetoric. This is a critical point: this means that for Barth homiletics is no longer a species of rhetoric, but a subfield of dogmatics. Barth shifts the frame from rhetoric to theology. Kay believes that given Barth's polemics it seems to drive "a stake into the heart of rhetoric," but in truth, Barth makes a dogmatic claim over rhetoric.[16]

Despite the tremendous preaching influence of Broadus, twentieth-century cracks emerged in the house of Enlightenment rationalism brought about by such voices as Harry Emerson Fosdick, R. E. C. Brown, and H. Grady Davis among others.[17] These preachers raised serious questions and forced rethinking about the dominant rational homiletical paradigm. Allen points out that forces outside of preaching, involving Martin Heidegger, Rudolph Bultmann, the new field of cultural studies, and the work of Marshall McLuhan and Walter Ong, helped contribute to the fact that the dominant deductive propositional approach to preaching, shaped by print media, were giving way to different approaches necessary for an oral culture. From the 1970s, the "New Homiletic" emerged as a major homiletical movement. The New Homiletic, by focusing on the hearer and the creation of an experience of the gospel through inductive method,

---

15. Kay, "Reorientation," 20.

16. Ibid., 21.

17. Harry Emerson Fosdick, "What's the Matter with Preaching?" (July 1928); the article is reprinted in *What's the Matter with Preaching Today?*, ed. Mike Graves (Louisville, KY: Westminster John Knox Press, 2004); R. E. C. Brown, *The Ministry of the Word* (London: SCM, 1958); H. Grady Davis, *Design for Preaching* (Philadelphia: Muhlenberg, 1958).

centrality of images, story, and narrative sermonic forms, was intentionally rhetorical. The New Homiletic was shaped principally by the work of five homileticians:

- Fred B. Craddock introduced the concept of inductive preaching.

- Charles Rice revived story and the gospel addressing human experience.

- Henry H. Mitchell developed the gospel addressing the whole person (experiential preaching) and celebration in preaching.

- Eugene Lowry advanced the homiletical plot, taking inductive movement and storytelling and shaping it into a concrete homiletical form.

- David Buttrick determined the way thought forms in a community's mind and developed a sermonic structure where the sermon flows in the same manner.

Though each of these scholars draws, in different ways and degrees, on the rhetorical tradition, David Buttrick sums up the overall rhetorical emphasis of the New Homiletic:

Designing a move [in a sermon] is not merely an exercise in rhetorical strategy. Obviously, preachers employ exegesis, theology, tradition, cultural analysis, and so forth in presenting ideas. Nevertheless, let us not disparage rhetoric. Rightly rhetoric is concerned with shaping moves in such a way that moves will fit human consciousness, and there contend with the social attitudes that people bring to church. Ideally, people should not tell that they are being talked to so much as having conceptual meaning form in consciousness as their own thought process. So designing moves involves theological smarts and rhetorical skill—trained rhetorical skill.[18]

Following the call of the New Homiletic to rhetorical preaching, homiletical scholars Lucy Lind Hogan and Robert Reid coauthored the aforementioned *Connecting with the Congregation: Rhetoric and the Art of Preaching*, and Reid presented, in 2006, an open essay at the Academy of

---

18. David Buttrick, *Homiletic: Moves and Structures* (Philadelphia: Fortress Press, 1987), 29.

Homiletics entitled "Homiletics Dancing at the Edge of Rhetoric," further summarizing his thinking on the relationship between rhetoric and homiletics.[19] Hogan and Reid summarize their purpose and essentially join preaching and rhetoric:

> The purpose of this book is to introduce students of preaching to the basic theory of the art of rhetoric as it applies to the task of preaching. We want to help preachers learn how to be intentional in thinking rhetorically about their homiletic task, to assist them in being able to adopt a rhetorical stance as part of a constructive theology of preaching.[20]

Hogan and Reid follow the rhetorical scholar Karlyn Kohrs Campbell in defining rhetoric as "the study of all the processes by which people influence each other through symbols, regardless of the intent or the source," therefore, rhetoric is concerned with "social truths, addressed to others, justified by reasons that reflect particular cultural values."[21]

Kohrs Campbell's view is that the human being can "never not communicate" because little that we say or do does not have persuasive effect or influence, and is therefore rhetorical. Kohrs Campbell distinguishes rhetoric from the rhetorical act. The rhetorical act is "an intentional, created, polished attempt to overcome the obstacles in a given situation with a specific audience on a given issue to achieve a particular end."[22] Hogan and Reid help to distinguish rhetoric and the rhetorical act by comparing the difference between *preaching* and a *sermon*:

> Preaching may be defined very broadly as the proclamation of good news. . . . Christians preach through words spoken in love, through acts of kindness and mercy, and when advocating justice. But when we speak of a sermon, we think of it in the same way that Kohrs Campbell describes a specific rhetorical act. A particular preacher delivers a sermon to a particular congregation during a particular worship service.

---

19. Hogan and Reid, *Connecting with the Congregation: Rhetoric and the Art of Preaching*, and Robert Stephen Reid, "Homiletics Dancing at the Edge of Rhetoric" (presented at the Academy of Homiletics, University of Dubuque, December 2006).

20. Hogan and Reid, *Connecting with the Congregation*, 21.

21. Ibid., 9.

22. Ibid., 11.

In this sense, the sermon functions as an "intentional, created, polished attempt to overcome the obstacles in a given situation."[23]

Following Wayne Booth, Hogan and Reid argue that preaching should take a "rhetorical stance." A rhetorical stance is to "maintain a proper balance between three elements that are at work in any communicative effort: the available arguments about the subject itself, the interests and peculiarities of the audience, and the voice, the implied character of the speaker."[24] Hogan and Reid support the contention by David Cunningham that all Christian theology is reasoning conducted by means of persuasive argument.[25] Booth argues that rhetoric and religion are essentially wedded and calls for "a constructive theology that stops toying with needing to emulate modernity's rationalism or to hide its discourse in tiny enclaves within divinity schools. He asks for a theology that refused to be embarrassed by the fact that its central claims are rhetorically established."[26]

Reid, in his 2006 essay, quotes Herbert Simons's book *The Rhetorical Turn: Invention and Persuasion in the Conduct of Inquiry*, the second of two collections of essays intended to give birth to what is now called the "Rhetoric of Inquiry" movement.[27] Simons and his colleagues openly acknowledge that knowledge is socially constructed, and therefore rhetorically rather logically derived. The turn involves the recognition by many scholars across all disciplines that reason is fundamentally rhetorical, and therefore, inquiry as argument and scholarship in the human sciences is basically a rhetorical enterprise of argument-making. The rhetorical turn is "the recognition that no body of inquiry can escape the fact that it conducts its talk and research by way of words and persuasion."[28] In preach-

---

23. Ibid., 11–12.

24. Ibid., 17.

25. David Cunningham, *Faithful Persuasion: In Aid of a Rhetoric of Christian Theology* (South Bend, IN: University of Notre Dame Press, 1991).

26. Hogan and Reid, *Connecting with the Congregation*, 19.

27. Herbert Simons, ed., *The Rhetorical Turn: Invention and Persuasion in the Conduct of Inquiry* (Chicago: University of Chicago Press, 1990).

28. Ibid., 19.

ing, this means that even divinely revealed truth must be contextualized in order to be received by the hearers. From this frame of reference, when Barth makes his argument for the primacy of theological efficacy of the word of God over and without rhetorical processes, he is using rhetorical processes to make his argument.

Furthermore, Reid suggested in his open essay that, despite the validity of the rhetorical turn, most of the field of homiletics still operated with a nineteenth-century view of rhetoric that treats the art as simple persuasion (separated from reasoning). Persuasion is taken up as the move one makes at the close of a sermon after making a structured argument. Reid summarizes his conclusion to this question of the relationship between homiletics and rhetoric by using the dance analogy: "Dancing with a partner requires keeping in step with and also not stepping on the partner's toes. The Divine-human dance is always afoot in preaching; theology must lead, but homiletics still needs to know what its dance partner (rhetoric) is thinking and how to keep from tripping over the steps it takes."[29]

Lucy Lind Hogan and Robert Reid represent a model of rhetorical homiletics, a partnership between homiletics and rhetoric.

Another significant step forward in the partnership between homiletics and rhetoric is the work of André Resner Jr. in *Preacher and Cross: Person in Message in Theology and Rhetoric*.[30] Resner continues our discussion by arguing that preaching can be analyzed according to two logically diverse frames of reference, theology and rhetoric. From the perspective of theology, God makes preaching effective, or efficacious, for the ends that God chooses regardless of preacher input at the level of ethos (preacher character/credibility), pathos (hearer emotionality), or logos (arrangement, style, or argument of the sermon). From the perspective of rhetoric, the preaching moment can be examined as any human speech. As such, the sermon is judged by its persuasiveness, which depends on how the audience perceives the preacher's credibility (ethos), whether and how the preacher moves the hearers (pathos), and whether the logic of the sermon

---

29. Robert Stephen Reid, "Homiletics Dancing at the Edge of Rhetoric," 10.

30. André Resner Jr., *Preacher and Cross: Person and Message in Theology and Rhetoric* (Grand Rapids: Wm. B. Eerdmans Publishing Co.), 1999.

is convincing (logos). The preacher is caught in a "pickle" between these two frames of rationality and perception. If the preacher wishes to operate solely from the theological vantage point, it can be perceived (a la Barth) that his or her person matters not at all—everything depends on God. But that can lead to what Resner calls a kind of "homiletical Docetism," where there is a disembodied word, one not made flesh among us this day. If the preacher, recognizing that hearers make human judgments about perceived preacher credibility (ethos), emotional appeal (pathos), and logical argument (logos), whether Barth likes it or not, and thus capitulates entirely to the rhetorical frame of reference in thinking about and practicing preaching, a new heretical probability arises, that of "homiletical Donatism." Resner describes this as the sin of holding the word's efficacy hostage to the perceived moral credibility of the preacher, but also to the preacher's oratorical and communicational skills.

Resner argues that the concept of "reverse-ethos" found in a careful reading of Paul can help to overcome this impasse:

> Reverse-ethos, then, is a theologically-informed rhetorical category which describes the preacher's person in the rhetorical situation of Christian proclamation. It is designed to "reverse" or "ironic" ethos to differentiate it from an Aristotelian notion of ethos which derives its meaning and function primarily from paying attention to audience expectation as to what makes a speaker credible.[31]

What makes the Apostle Paul credible is the word of the cross and not the hearers. Hearer expectation is often based in *kata sarka* (ways of knowing according to the flesh), and for Paul, this is the heart of the problem of the Corinthian church with his ministry. The Corinthians viewed Paul's ministry from the perspective of the way of knowing from the flesh (i.e., according to the categories they had inherited from the culture, especially those of rhetorical analysis). As a result, they, based in *kata sarka*, compared Paul's preaching to the preaching of Apollos. Because of the gospel of Jesus Christ crucified, Paul's way of knowing was *kata stauron* (according to the cross), that is, the death/resurrection of Christ and daily death/

---

31. Ibid., 4.

life of the disciple. For Paul, the cross effected both a way of being as well as a new epistemology—a new way of knowing and judging. Therefore, the Corinthian church could not judge his ministry correctly if they only used their former ways of knowing (*kata sarka*). Only God could truly and ultimately judge (1 Cor 5:2-5), because God judges Paul and the Christian's life *kata stauron*, that is, according to the cross. According to Resner, "The message of the cross puts to death *kata sarka* standards of what makes preaching preaching, what makes preachers preachers."[32]

For Paul, all preaching is dependent on God. Yet, the person of the preacher is critical to the delivery of the message and can obscure the message. Preaching *kata stauron* is that the efficacy of preaching is reliant upon God, and the preacher's life is important as a crucified life. When the preacher preaches the cross, the message of the cross covers the weakness of the preacher's life. The message of the cross embodies both the kerygma (the message) and the keryx (herald), because the cross subverts the world's standards for credibility, status, privilege, power, and position into Christ's standards, which are evident in servanthood, lowly service, weakness, death, and hardship. The message of the cross is not changed by the weakness of the preacher, because the weakness of the preacher is the message, that is, the weaknesses of the world and human life overcome by the weakness of the cross. Paul's message of the cross resolves the homiletical Donatism versus homiletical Docetism polarization because reverse ethos as a theologically formed rhetorical category reverses the Aristotelian notion of ethos as paying attention to audience expectation and turns the preacher first to the cross as the message of Christian proclamation. In my view, Resner's work, based upon grounding his concept of reverse-ethos in the biblical text, concludes the matter of articulating the relevance of rhetorical and theological homiletics for Christian preaching, and the African American preaching tradition has a significant and valuable contribution to make to the discussion as well.

I would like to make several summary comments based upon our discussion of the historical relationship between rhetoric and homiletics in Western preaching. A significant portion of African American preaching

---

32. Ibid., 115.

has always been in the oral tradition of inductive, narrative, imagistic, and storied language. Despite the fact that a portion of African American preaching tradition adopted the preaching form of European Enlightenment rationalism, the majority of the tradition has functioned more akin to the oral genius of the African American folk preaching tradition. In many ways, the New Homiletic movement of the twentieth century moved in the direction of the oral nature of the majority of African American preaching as Cleophus J. LaRue makes this argument in his article "Two Ships Passing in the Night."[33]

Second, I believe that homiletical rhetoric is essential in this twenty-first-century digital and oral age as never before, and therefore means slightly loosening preaching from its Barthian theological base. We live in a postmodern, postcolonial, and poststructuralist age, and fewer and fewer people regard the Christian Bible "as the final, authoritative *truth* . . . with the Holy Spirit as the witness and therefore no need to persuade an audience."[34] More and more persuasion is necessary, given the competing claims for truth and the lack of predominance of the Christian faith in America and around the world. The Christian preacher is forced to persuade if the gospel is to be relevant in this contemporary global culture, or Christianity will become an enclaved faith with a few sectarian adherents.

Finally, to this point in homiletical scholarship, the dialogue between preaching and rhetoric has been mainly carried on as a discussion of European or Euro-American homiletical perspectives. In chapter 1, we discussed several scholars of African American preaching who utilized Aristotelian rhetorical categories of logos, pathos, and ethos. It is also clear that many African American speakers utilize rhetorical technique, such as proofs and evidence, anaphora, alliteration, metaphor, epistrophe, antithesis, argumentation, intonation, and so forth. Euro-centric and African American preachers alike—or any good preacher regardless of race, nationality, gender, or gender preference—utilize sound rhetorical prin-

---

33. See Cleophus J. LaRue, "Two Ships Passing in the Night," in *What's the Matter with Preaching Today?*, 127–44.

34. Hogan and Reid, *Connecting with the Congregation: Rhetoric and the Art of Preaching*, 24.

ciples. What is distinctive is that rhetorical processes are fundamental to African American preaching, and not something that one adds on after the preacher has figured out the rational content of what to say. Theological and rhetorical processes are not two unique steps in the preparation process. As we will discuss now, it will be clear that the rhetorical as well as the theological enterprise is at the heart of the African American preaching tradition—that one does not add on rhetoric after one has made a structured argument. My goal is to clarify and deepen the understanding of rhetorical processes in African American preaching. Let me now discuss Zora Neale Hurston and Henry Louis Gates as critical foundations through which rhetorical processes in African American preaching can be understood.

ZORA NEALE HURSTON AND THE ORAL TRADITION OF BLACK PREACHING

Zora Neale Hurston (1901–1960) was a civil rights activist, folklorist, novelist, anthropologist, ethnographer, and "Genius of the South."[35] She was one of the important figures of the Harlem Renaissance of the 1920s and 1930s before writing her most critically acclaimed book, *Their Eyes Were Watching God*. Based upon extensive anthropological research and compilations of Southern black oral traditions, she became a critical interpreter of black culture and black ways of being in America. Hurston's four novels, two books of folklore, autobiography, short stories, and plays are an invaluable source on the rhetoric of oral cultures of African Americans. She and her work were virtually forgotten until, in 1975, *Ms. Magazine* published Alice Walker's essay "In Search of Zora Neale Hurston" that revived interest in the author.[36]

The Sanctified Church (1981), a posthumous edition assembling various essays on folklore, legend, and popular black mythology first published between the late 1920s and the early 1940s, is particularly helpful in our

---

35. In 1973, the words "Novelist," "Folklorist," and "A Genius of the South" were placed on the marker erected at Zora Neale Hurston's grave in Eatonville, Florida, by Alice Walker.

36. Alice Walker's essay "In Search of Zora Neale Hurston" was republished in Walker's book *In Search of Our Mothers' Gardens* (New York: Mariner Books; repr., 2003), as "Looking for Zora," 93–118.

discussion of the importance of rhetoric in African American preaching.[37] According to M. Cooper Harris,

> The essays in *The Sanctified Church* explore the semiotic complexities of black churches through their worship, interrogated and understood as cultural performance. Hurston suggests that the Negro "self" is permeated by a vital sense of "drama," that expressions of meaning "rich in metaphor and simile" are consistently depicted in intricate and ubiquitous interaction rituals transpiring in the course of every day living.[38]

Hurston argues that black people in America, deriving from a cultural history originating in West Africa, have a legacy of an oral tradition, that is, the spoken word and oral transmission of tales, music, dance, proverbs, beliefs, sermons, and so on. This is different than the cultural history of the Western world, which is principally preserved and transmitted based upon the written word, and hence could be called textual.

To contrast oral and textual worldviews, Hurston suggests that language is analogous to money. In primitive communities, actual goods were bartered and exchanged for what one wanted. This finally evolved into a coin. The coin is not real wealth, but a symbol of wealth. Eventually, the coin was abandoned for legal tender, paper money, and then later checks. People with highly developed textual languages have words structured as detached ideas to describe things—"that which we squat on" becomes "chair" and then in scholarly circles, "chair" becomes even further abstracted to "chairness." In textual language, words are often abstracted to describe reality, such as "ideation" and "pleonastic." Hurston calls this "legal tender," and scholarly words are an example of "check words," as well as great literature, such as *Paradise Lost* and *Sartar Resartus*.

Hurston suggests that the words of African Americans are action words and not principally abstractions. The African American's very interpretation of the English language is in terms of pictures, which results in

---

37. Zora Neale Hurston, *The Sanctified Church: The Folklore Writings of Zora Neale Hurston* (Berkeley, CA: Turtle Island Foundation, 1981).

38. M. Cooper Harris, "The Preacher in the Text: Zora Neale Hurston and the Homiletics of Literature," University of Chicago Web Forum, February, 2008, https://divinity.uchicago.edu/sites/default/files/imce/pdfs/webforum/022008/harriss.pdf.

rich metaphor and simile. She believes that pictures are easier to explain because "action came before speech." The oral tradition of African Americans uses words that are "close-fitting"—words that action must be added to, such as "sitting-chair," or "cook-pot," because according to Hurston, every speaker has in their mind the picture of the object in use. Hurston admits that much of this has been influenced by the acculturation of African Americans into mainstream American life, but oral traditions still heavily remain in black culture. For Hurston, Western culture thinks in a written language, and African Americans think in word pictures like the hieroglyphics of Ancient Egypt.

According to Hurston, the Negro is famous world over for "imitation" and "mimicry." This mimicry is not based in feelings of inferiority, as so many have argued, and does not harm the Negro's standing as an original. Imitation is fundamental to all great art, and indeed is the nature of all art—even Shakespeare. Negro mimicry is, then, the evidence of something that permeates the Negro self, "drama." Hurston gives an example of a ritual of drama that might occur in thousands of cities, indicative of black life everywhere and based upon the social interactions of the community:

> A Negro girl strolls past the corner lounger. Her whole body panging and posing. A slight shoulder movement that calls attention to her bust, that is all of a dare. A hippy undulation below the waist that is a sheaf of promises tied with conscious power. She is acting out "I'm a darned sweet woman and you know it."[39]

Hurston argues, as an example, that this kind of drama has a male counterpart and many similar such rituals are operative in black communal life. Whenever black people act in their own interest, and as an expression of the conscious black self, the action is embellished. Therefore, she suggests that black religious services are "prose poetry," and the "prayers and sermons are polished until they are true works of art.... The beauty of the Old Testament does not exceed that of a Negro prayer."[40] Drama is a natural and inherent part of African American life in America, and

---

39. Hurston, *The Sanctified Church*, 50.
40. Ibid., 54.

therefore African American life and expression is naturally and inherently performative and rhetorical.

Hurston articulates a theory of black narration, inclusive of all oral telling, including black preaching, and identifies components of this artistry by setting forth what she calls "characteristics of Negro expression." Preaching is our main focus, and therefore, I have set Hurston's characteristics in terms of preaching. First, she identifies "drama"—the preacher's words are action words and interpretations of the English language in terms of pictures. Second, "illustration"—the preacher uses vivid illustration because it is easier to illustrate than explain because action came before speech. Third, "the will to adorn"—the preacher decorates and embroiders narration with figurative language with the intent to satisfy "the desire for beauty" in the preacher's and congregation's soul. In the will to adorn, Hurston argues that black people's greatest contribution to the English language is the making over of the English language through the use of metaphor and simile.

Hurston includes in *The Sanctified Church* an artifact of Negro expression, a recorded sermon from May 3, 1929, by C. C. Lovelace at Eau Gallie, Florida, "The Wounds of Jesus." The text of the sermon is Zechariah 13:6 (NIV), "If someone asks, 'What are these wounds on your body?' they will answer, 'The wounds I was given at the house of my friends.'" The point of the sermon is Jesus is wounded in the house of his friends, saving the world from sin. Lovelace is bringing the sermon to climax, and intones Jesus dying on the cross:

> He died until the great belt in the wheel of time
> And de geological strata fell aloose
> And a thousand angels rushed to de canopy of heben
> With flaming swords in their hands
> And placed their feet upon blue ether's bosom and looked back at de dazzling throne
> And de arc angels had veiled their faces
> And de throne was draped in mournin
> And de orchestra had struck silent for the space of half an hour
> Angels had lifted their harps to de weepin willows

> And God had looked off to-wards immensity
> And blazin worlds fell off His teeth
> And about that time Jesus groaned on de cross and said, "It is finished."
> And then de chambers of hell explode....[41]

For Hurston, this is Negro expression at its best—poetry, imagery, metaphor, simile, word pictures, summarized as drama, illustration, and the will to adorn.

Hurston foregrounds, in many of her works, particularly *Their Eyes Were Watching God* and *Jonah's Vine Gourd*, the personhood, struggles, and yet beautiful and poetic language of these dramatic, often unlettered preachers. So much so that she was criticized for emphasizing preachers and their sermons as literary and rhetorical devices. The *New York Times* reviewed *Jonah's Vine Gourd* and said that John Pearson's final sermon was "too good, too brilliantly splashed with poetic imagery, to be the product of any one Negro preacher." Hurston responds in a letter written to James Weldon Johnson: "There are hundreds of preachers who are equaling that sermon weekly.... [The preacher] must also be an artist. He must be both a poet and an actor of a very high order.... They are the first artists, the ones intelligible to the masses."[42] In a May 12 letter to Lewis Gannett, who reviewed *Jonah's Gourd Vine* for the *New York Herald-Tribune*, she writes, "The greatest poets among us are in our pulpits and the greatest poetry has come out of them. It is merely not set down. It passes from mouth to mouth as in the days of Homer."[43] Hurston emphasized the originality and artfulness of black expression, especially in preaching form, noting that it can be compared to Homer, the first and greatest of the epic poets, and noted source of the Western canon.

Along with oral traditions from Africa, I want to turn to another perspective as to why African American preaching is inherently and naturally rhetorical: the institution of slavery and its attendant historical and contemporary racist manifestations helped the formation of rhetorical

---

41. Ibid., 95–102.
42. Cooper Harris, "The Preacher in the Text," 22.
43. Ibid., 22.

processes in black communal life, the most critical of which Henry Louis Gates suggests is the "master trope" of black life in America, "signifying."

SIGNIFYING AND AFRICAN AMERICAN PREACHING

I learned the rhetorical strategies of signifying as an adolescent. I was taught the language of standard English for navigation through Euro-American culture for the purposes of survival, school exams, standardized tests, proper manners, decency, etiquette, and especially for future advancement in life. Correspondingly, I was taught and intuited in the home, church, and neighborhood a second language that black people shared for privileged meanings among themselves, the language of indirection, innuendo, double meanings, and black identity that we called "signifying." From the art of signifying, I learned improvisation, ad-lib quickness, verbal dexterity, persuasion, and creative expression. Yet, I am in agreement with the comment of Henry Louis Gates that analyzing signifying is like "stumbling unaware into a hall of mirrors."[44]

Signifying is so fundamental to black life, and so familiar of a rhetorical practice that one would think it would be easy to write about as an African American scholar. In fact, it is difficult to bring a concept that is so second nature to black vernacular into the standards of scholarly discourse. As a result, Gates says that he encounters "the great resistance of inertia when writing about it." I clearly understand and overwhelmingly concur with Gates that because of such familiarity, it is very difficult to define signifying. D. G. Myers, in an article about Henry Louis Gates's classic work on signifying, *The Signifying Monkey*, comments on Gates's inability to define signifying. Myers argues that though Gates devotes twenty-five pages to defining it, he does little more than gather the definitions of others such as Mezz Mezzrow and Zora Neale Hurston.[45] Myers suggests that

---

44. Henry Louis Gates Jr., *The Signifying Monkey: Theory of African American Literary Criticism* (New York: Oxford Press, 1988), 44.

45. See D. G. Myers, "Signifying Nothing," *New Criterion* (February 1990), http://www.newcriterion.com/articles.cfm/Sound-and-fury-5627. According to jazz musician Mezz Mezzrow, to signify is to "hint, to put on an act, boast, make a gesture." The novelist Zora Neale Hurston defines signifying as "a contest in hyperbole carried on for no other reason."

these conceptions of signifying sound similar to a traditional category of rhetoric known as "epideictic," where—in some definitions—language is used for display whose sole purpose is to showcase the orator's gifts. Myers concludes that to assimilate black signifying to the "Eurocentric" tradition of classical rhetoric is to lose "what we might think of as the discrete black difference." Gates takes pains to track the concept to Africa instead.[46]

In complete fairness to Gates, signifying is hard to define, not only because of intuitive familiarity, and difficulties of translation of black vernacular into concepts of standard English, but also the many variances and the continual evolving practices of signifying in the black community. When Gates says that analyzing signifying is like "stumbling unaware into a hall of mirrors," he means signifying is an indirect communicative art, and by the very nature of its nature, it resists traditional scholarly definition. Signifying can only be defined through possibilities of indirection and innuendo because signifying, at its heart, *is* indirection and innuendo. In other words, one has to signify to define signifying. Gates, in the attempt to define signifying, gathers many definitions by scholars, then critically comments on their various definitions and suggests his almost definition: in effect, definition by indirection and innuendo—signifying.

Scholars suggest, among many definitions, that signifying is an indirect African American rhetorical form, strategy, and stance, a means of cultural self-definition, and for Gates, a critical means to explore the African American literary tradition.[47] Gates writes that the first scholar

---

46. Ibid.
47. R. D. Abrahams, *Talking Black* (Rowley, MA: Newbury House, 1976); T. Kochman, "Toward an Ethnography of Black American Speech Behavior," in *Rappin' and Stylin' Out: Communication in Urban America*, ed. T. Kochman (Urbana: University of Illinois Press, 1972); G. Smitherman, *Talkin and Testifyin: The Language of Black America* (New York: Holt, Rinehart, and Winston, 1977); C. Mitchell-Kernan, "Signifiying as a Form of Verbal Art," in *Mother Wit from the Laughing Barrel: Readings in the Interpretation of Africa-American Folklore*, ed. A. Dundes (Englewood Cliff, NJ: Prentice-Hall, 1973); T. Garner, "Understanding Oral Rhetorical Practices in African American Cultural Relationships," in *Towards Achieving Maat*, ed. V. J. Duncan (Dubuque, IA: Kendall/Hunt Publishing, 1998).

to define both signifying and the ritual itself was Zora Neale Hurston.[48] Hurston characterizes, in *Mules and Men*, the ritual of signifying, and then explains the word *signify* as a means of "showing off," rhetorically:

> "Talking 'bout dogs," put in Gene Oliver, "they got plenty sense. Nobody can't fool dogs much."
>
> "And speaking 'bout hams," cut in Big Sweet meaningly, "if Joe Willard don't stay out of dat bunk he was in last night, Ah'm gonter springle some salt down his back and sugar-cure *his* hams."
>
> Joe snatched his pole out of the water with a jerk and glared at Big Sweet who stood sidewise looking at him most pointedly.
>
> "Aw, woman, quit tryin' to signify."
>
> "Ah kin signify all Ah please, Mr. Nappy-Chin, so long as Ah know what Ah'm talking about."[49]

Hurston clearly demonstrates double meaning, indirection, and innuendo here, and is the first to demonstrate that women, as a rhetorical strategy of self-definition and vehicle of liberation, signify on men.[50]

Thurman Garner and Carolyn Calloway-Thomas define signifying as "an example of what we find when African American voices are foregrounded for a Black presence."[51] Signifying is a rhetorical strategy whose purpose is to empower cultural definition by claiming space for black presence. This is why rhetoric is not an appendage after the preacher has

---

48. Gates devotes an entire chapter in *The Signifying Monkey* to Zora Neale Hurston and the concept of the "speakerly text." Gates defines a "speakerly text" as a text whose rhetorical strategy is designed to represent an oral literary tradition, designed to emulate "the phonetic, grammatical, and lexical patterns of actual speech and produce the 'illusion of oral narration.'" Hurston's text *Mules and Men* is the first in the African American tradition. See "Zora Neale Hurston and the Speakerly Text," (170–216).

49. Zora Neale Hurston, *Mules and Men: Negro Folklore Tales and Voodoo Practices in the South* (New York: Harper & Row, 1970), 161.

50. Gates, *The Signifying Monkey*, 182.

51. Thurman Garner and Carolyn Calloway-Thomas, "African American Orality: Expanding Rhetoric," in *Understanding African American Rhetoric: Classical Origins to Contemporary Innovations*, ed. Ronald L. Jackson II and Elaine B. Richardson (New York: Routledge, 2003), 53.

decided the rational content of what to say: signifying and the like are verbal jabs and rhetorical feints to validate personhood, identity, and a sense of being in a world that, in whatever form, seeks to deny fundamental aspects of being human. Richard Lischer argues that "signifying was the only mode of communication, other than suicidal confrontation, that was available to an oppressed people."[52] As I read Lischer's comment, I remembered, as an example, the words of centuries of signifying African American preachers: "Everybody talking about heaven ain't going there." In mixed company of slave master and slaves in worship, slaves knew the preacher was talking about the slave master, who though they talked and sang about heaven, because of their practice of slavery, were not going there. Later, I will signify and summarily make the argument that signifying is an overlooked rhetorical strategy of the African American preaching tradition.

Though not able to define signifying with certitude, Gates has made major contributions to the study of African American rhetoric by combining rhetoric with sociolinguistic analysis of black discourse to suggest that language must be studied in use, hence Gates's commitment to study black vernacular in the African American literary tradition. Rhetoric, for Gates, means tropes, and tropes are regarded as constitutive of language. A trope is, literally, a turn—turning words away from their literal to a metaphorical meaning for the purpose of rhetorical effect. Gates identifies signifying as the "master trope," "the trope of tropes" of black rhetoric. For Gates, signifying is inclusive of traditional rhetorical categories such as repetition, rhyming, hyperbole, irony, synecdoche, several forms of persuasion, insult, boasting, and lying—all by means of innuendo or indirection. Signifying is "a linguistic masking, the verbal sign of the mask of blackness that demarcates the boundary between the white linguistic realm and the black, two domains that exist side by side in a homonymic relation signified by the very concept of signification."[53]

---

52. Richard Lischer, *The Preacher King: Martin Luther King, Jr. and the Word That Moved America* (New York: Oxford University Press, 1995), 156.

53. Patricia Bizzell and Bruce Herzberg, *The Rhetorical Tradition: Readings from Classical Times to the Present*, Henry Louis Gates, "The Signifying Monkey and the Language of Signifying: Rhetorical Difference and the Orders of Meaning" (Boston: Bedford/St. Martin's, Second Edition, 2001), 1571.

While several scholars have used the terms *signifying* and *playing the dozens* interchangeably, Gates is careful to delineate that "dozens" is a subform of signifying. Gates points out that many scholars focus on the aggressive ritual of "dozens," rather than seeing the concept of signifying as a whole, and credits Claudia Mitchell-Kernan with understanding that signifying is an overall "pervasive mode of language use rather than one specific verbal game."[54]

To help with the distinction between signifying overall and "playing the dozens," let me explain "the dozens."[55] The name "dozens" probably derives from an eighteenth-century meaning of the verb *dozen*, "to stupefy, daze" through language.[56] "Dozens" is a verbal contest, in which two people compete in a head-to-head competition of "trash talking." The ritual involves taking turns insulting, or "crackin" or "dissin" on each other or their adversary's mother or other family members, until one of them is stunned and has no comeback, or even worse, gets angry. The object of the game is to bewilder and confound one's opponent with swift and skillful speech based on verbal creativity and dexterity. It is a contest of personal and rhetorical power—of wit, self-control, verbal ability, emotional strength, mental agility, and mental toughness. Each verbal jab has the effect of upping the ante. The first one to anger is the loser. Defeat can be humiliating; but a skilled contender, win or lose, may gain respect.

In my book *American Dream 2.0: A Christian Way Out of the Great Recession*, I discuss the "dozens" as a rhetorical lens through which to view the highly anticipated April 2008 rhetorical performance of Jeremiah A. Wright Jr. at the National Press Club in Washington, DC.[57] In the midst of a media-created firestorm based upon sound bites from his sermons that created controversy, which for many threatened the presidential aspirations of Barack Obama, Wright gave a clear and insightful lecture and explanation of what Wright termed the "unknown phenomenon of the

---

54. Ibid., 80, and Claudia Mitchell-Kernan, "Signifying, Loud Talking, and Marking," in Kochman, *Rappin' and Stylin' Out: Communication in Urban Black America*, 315–36.

55. See "Dozens," *Urban Dictionary*, www.urbandictionary.com/define.php?term=dozens.

56. Peter Tamary in Robert S. Gold, *Jazz Talk* (New York: Bobbs-Merrill, 1975), 76.

57. Frank A. Thomas, *American Dream 2.0: A Christian Way Out of the Great Recession* (Nashville: Abingdon Press, 2012), 71–90.

black church." In the question-and-answer session, Wright's mood and tenor changed. He shifted into the dozens, summed up by reporter Amy Sullivan Washington, who suggested Wright "transformed into a defiant, derisive figure, snapping one-liners at the unfortunate moderator tasked with reading the questions and stepping back with a grin on his face after each and every one, clearly enjoying himself.[58]

In explaining his shift to verbal confrontation (dozens) during the question-and-answer session, Wright pointed to the fact that after delivering a critical lecture on the history and traditions of the black church, the questions from the press were related, not to the lecture, but to the media's characterizations—as if Wright had not spoken at all.[59] The media's questions again rendered Wright invisible, and Wright utilized the dozens to claim rhetorical space for black identity in the midst of the perception of hostile Euro-centric forces.

Most often, though, the dozens happen in the street, some would argue, the place of the most complex conversation-performance in the black community. Bizzell and Hertzberg suggest exchanges on the street have three purposes: to exchange information; to enact social relationships of friendship, kinship, and business; and to establish the speaker's social status:

> The street is the scene of verbal play (mostly male), which, even when it creates solidarity, has a competitive edge. Street exchanges establish the

---

58. Amy Sullivan Washington, "Jeremiah Wright Goes to War," *Time*, April 28, 2008, http://content.time.com/time/politics/article/0,8599,1735662,00.html.

59. In an interview with the author, Wright pointed out that the mood shift had to do with the obvious and total "dissing" of his scholarly presentation and the continued apparent "dissing" of the Black Religious Experience. Wright suggested that his presentation was the first of several powerful and professional presentations on "The Prophetic Witness of the Black Church" given at a three-day conference sponsored by the Samuel De Witt Proctor's Pastor's Conference. Following Wright's presentation that morning, there were papers presented by John W. Kinney, the dean of the School of Theology at the Samuel DeWitt Proctor School of Theology at Virginia Union University and president of the Association of Theological Schools, Katie Cannon, one of the country's leading Womanist theologians and professor at Union Theological Seminary, and Dwight Hopkins, professor of theology at the University of Chicago Divinity School—papers that echoed the presentation made by Wright in his opening presentation. The professional papers were followed by two days of panel discussion held by professors and graduate students at the Howard University School of Divinity.

speaker's reputation in the community. Where status on economic or educational achievement is problematic, especially for men, the ability to rap, to establish dominance, camaraderie, solidarity, and opposition to white hegemony, as well as to entertain, is the measure of communal admiration. In black communities, linguistic virtuosity is highly prized.[60]

Gates suggests H. Rap Brown as a master of "black vernacular rhetorical games," and his understanding of signifying is unsurpassed by any scholar. Brown said, "We played the Dozens like white folks play Scrabble." Brown insisted that both men and women play the dozens and some of the best "were girls." Dozens was "unrelentingly mean because what you try to do is destroy someone with words," but signifying was more humane because "instead of coming down on someone's mother, you come down on them." Whereas the dozens were structured to make one's subject feel bad, Brown says, "Signifying allowed you a choice—you could either make a cat feel good or bad. If you had just destroyed someone [verbally] or if they were just down already, signifying could help them over."[61]

Again, these rhetorical processes and skills are not the add-ons of persuasion after one has figured out the rational content of what to say. These rhetorical processes are at the very heart of communication, based in the need and desire to establish identity personhood, social status, and ultimately a place in the human family. Many have a hard time understanding how such verbal battles lead to violence, and even death. It is because in an environment hostile to the very nature of one's being, if the speaker's verbal quest to claim identity, personhood, and social status is denied, or the perception of denial is operative, too often the struggle is raised to the level of life and death violence.

Often, the dozens in a hostile and combative environment involves personal insult and the attempt to verbally injure and embarrass. But there are times when the signifying is nonpersonal, and as a result, becomes fun, humorous, and comedic. An example of this occurred during the

---

60. Patricia Bizzell and Bruce Herzberg, *The Rhetorical Tradition: Readings from Classical Times to the Present*, 2nd ed. (Boston, MA: Bedford/St. Martin's, 2001), 1546.

61. Gates, *The Signifying Monkey*, 73.

2014 Ford Neighborhood Awards Show, hosted by comedian and television personality Steve Harvey. A spontaneous "battle" broke out between Lavelle Crawford and Mr. Brown (David Mann).[62] The "battlers" laughed, cajoled, and made fun of each other's physical appearance, but it was in fun and laughter, and everyone had a good time. It was signifying as entertainment, a critical expression of black life in an often-hostile world.

Mitchell-Kernan, from her research, gives an example to illustrate the absence of negative import in signifying. An African American female, Grace, reports to Mitchell-Kernan that she has four children and swore not to have any more. She became pregnant, and because she was disgusted, didn't tell anybody. She started to show, and her sister Rochelle came over. Grace reports this interchange:

> Rochelle: Girl, you sure do need to join the Metrecal for lunch bunch.
>
> Grace: (noncommittally) Yea, I guess I am putting on a little weight.
>
> Rochelle: Now look here, girl, we both standing here soaking wet and you still trying to tell me it ain't raining.[63]

Mitchell-Kernan reports that Grace found the incident amusing and reports it as evidence of Rochelle's clever use of words in signifying. Her sister let her know, in a humorous way, that she knew she was pregnant. Rochelle was teasing, funny, and clever in what could have ended in insult, anger, or denial if spoken to directly. The choice of indirection and innuendo and their relationship allowed both people the opportunity to treat Rochelle's knowledge jokingly.

Mitchell-Kernan maintains that for the black community, "signifying is clearly thought of as a kind of art—a clever way of conveying messages. In fact, it does not lose its artistic merit even when it is malicious. It takes some skill to construct message with multi-level meanings, and sometimes

---

62. "Lavell Crawford Battles Mr. Brown and Kirk Franklin @ Hoodie Awards," www.youtube.com/watch?v=IyPN6M5JIw0&list=RDIyPN6M5JIw0#t=286.

63. Mitchell-Kernan, "Signifying, Loud Talking, and Marking," 322–23.

it takes equal expertise to unravel the puzzle presented in all of its many implications."[64]

When signifying is considered as a kind of art, a clever way of conveying messages, it is also a significant component of African American preaching. The role of signifying in African American preaching is often overlooked, and totally neglected by Gates, as Cooper-Harris comments: "Curiously, Gates ignores what may well comprise the richest of vernacular traditions in African-American culture: preachers and their sermons."[65] In her writings, Hurston foreground preachers and their sermons and "reminds us that preaching is to African-American literature what the Homeric tradition is to the Western canon."[66] Though outside the scope of this article, more study of the "preacherly rhetoric" of Hurston has the potential to bear rich fruit for understandings of African American preaching. When preaching is viewed as being characteristic of, in Hurston's words, "Negro expression," we can clearly see that preaching is inherently rhetorical and theological.

African American preaching, characteristic of "Negro expression," is about the use of metaphor, simile, hyperbole, and rhetorical strategies to convey messages that point beyond what can normally be described in the rational use of language. Because in some sense, these are universal rhetorical strategies, these characteristics can be seen in many other preaching traditions. African Americans' preaching, based in the oral traditions of West Africa, and the experience of slavery and the institutions of racism in America is, in the words of Hurston, "dramatic." This means that African American preaching has more heavily than any other American preaching tradition embellished the sermon with metaphor, simile, vivid illustration, and the will to adorn—all based in a word-picture view of reality. And how could it be otherwise, given minority status in an oppressive culture, and based upon the fact that persuasion was virtually the only viable emancipation option. Practically, armed revolution and violence have never been possible, or the most effective

---

64. Ibid., 323.

65. Cooper-Harris, "The Preacher in the Text," 2.

66. Ibid., 24.

means, to ensure liberation, human, and civil rights; therefore, moral and legal protest and persuasion have been the chief means to advance the claims of freedom.

In the historical and contemporary moment, the black preacher signified to establish rhetorical and theological space for black presence. The preacher signified against the devil, signified against institutions of racism and racists, in order to deliver the people into life-giving meanings and values. Sometimes, even in the pulpit, the preacher played the dozens against forces hostile to black life and personhood. The dozens in the pulpit is not done with the casual obscenity that usually accompanies it on the street, but the dozens are played nonetheless. Jeremiah A. Wright Jr. clearly illustrated dozens in his preaching that was "discovered" by the white media. Many of the excerpts that were taken out of context in his sermons were playing the dozen on America and its racism.

The preacher has sometimes signified on God, and in other times, signified on behalf of God. Words based in rational argument alone, with persuasion as a tag on, were never enough to give life to African American people, and so with the dramatic tools of invention, mimicry, and originality, the black preacher delivered a word of hope to the people. It was never enough to speak to the existential condition of the people to develop the rational content of the argument, and then add persuasion as rhetorical techniques. When Hamlet wanted to discern the truth of his father's death, he decided that indirection and innuendo would be best to elicit visible proof of what his father's ghost had told him. Hamlet said:

I'll have grounds
More relative than this—the play's the thing
Wherein I'll catch the conscience of the King.[67]

Hamlet would write the details of his father's death into a play, and then watch to see the response of Claudius the king (his father's murderer). Characteristic of Negro expression, and black preaching as a part

---

67. William Shakespeare, *Hamlet*, act 2, scene 2, 603–5.

of Negro expression, signifying, metaphor, simile, indirection, and innuendo and such captures the conscience of a person, community, or nation. Mitchell-Kernan sums up the matter when she says:

> Signifying operates so delightfully because apparent meaning serves as a key which directs hearers to some shared knowledge, attitudes, and values of signals that reference must be produced metaphorically.... Cleverness used in directing the attention of the hearer and audience to this shared knowledge upon which a speaker's artistic talent is judged.[68]

Finally, despite such intimate discussion of signifying for these many pages, it did not dawn on me, until writing the last words of this chapter, how much signifying was formation for my preaching. If there were more time and space, I would explore those connections to further buttress the argument that preaching is inherently rhetorical and theological. While signifying is hard to define, the fact that it helped to form my preaching ministry is some of the underpinning of my belief that preaching is inherently rhetorical and theological.

In this chapter, I discussed my perspective on the contribution of the African American preaching tradition to Western homiletical discussions as to whether preaching is a rhetorical or theological act. I concluded that black preaching, as part of Hurston's Negro expression, and Gates's signifying, is inherently rhetorical and theological. Black preaching was set in the overall context of black vernacular and discourse in America. In the next chapter, I will apply rhetorical theory and approaches to a sermon from the "Dean of Black Preaching," Gardner C. Taylor, entitled "His Own Clothes," in order to reflect upon the question, what is black preaching?

---

68. Henry Louis Gates Jr., "The Signifying Monkey and the Language of Signifyin(g): Rhetorical Difference and the Orders of Meaning," in Bizzell and Herzberg, *The Rhetorical Tradition: Readings from Classical Times to the Present*, 1579.

Chapter Three
"IT'S ALRIGHT NOW":

A Rhetorical Analysis of Gardner C. Taylor's Sermon "His Own Clothes"

In the introduction, I mentioned that as part of my research for this book, I convened separately twenty-two homileticians, who teach and publish scholarship on African American preaching, and twenty-five African American pastors, who practice preaching to congregations on a weekly basis. I followed a similar format in both discussions and asked each group to respond to the same three important and critical questions concerning African American preaching. Of the three questions, the one that is relevant for this chapter is this: What is black preaching?

In regard to both groups, we did not settle the question of defining exactly what black preaching is. As a matter of fact, we concluded that we were not sure that the question would ever be definitively settled once and for all. We resolved that each generation of pastors and scholars must wrestle with the question and make a contribution to the definition of this elusive and yet potent tradition. We acknowledged that the African American preaching tradition has been shaped by faithful responses to centuries of racial, sexual, social, cultural, political, economic, and gender oppression, and as a result, is uniquely able to minister to all people, and especially hurting and oppressed people, in America and all over the globe. But, for the most part, a definition was hard to pin down. In this chapter, I would like to offer my contribution to the discussion through the application of critical methods from the field of rhetoric, namely rhetorical criticism, to an actual preached sermon.

To begin, I will discuss the traditional homiletical model of understanding African American preaching by a discussion of primarily theological and traditional characteristics of black preaching. Scholars have already done much work in this area, and therefore, I will only briefly summarize and highlight several important characteristics.[1] Then, continuing in theological discourse, I will discuss the distinctiveness of African American preaching per the homiletical parameters of black preaching as outlined by homiletician Kenyatta Gilbert, the "rhetorical performative homiletics" of Henry H. Mitchell, and the "theological-hermeneutical" lens of Cleophus J. LaRue. Next, I will shift to the field of rhetoric and introduce two rhetorical critical approaches, close reading and ideological criticism, as the method of analysis of Gardner C. Taylor's sermon "His Own Clothes." Gardner C. Taylor is a paradigmatic example of the best of black preaching. Finally, I will apply these rhetorical approaches to the sermon and conclude with reflections on what is black preaching.

CHARACTERISTICS OF AFRICAN AMERICAN PREACHING

When we consider characteristics of the African American preaching tradition, I would argue that there are at least seven: the centrality of the Bible, the importance of experiential preaching, existential exegesis, inspiration of the Holy Spirit, suspense that leads to celebration, the call and response nature of the sermon, and the performative nature of the sermon.[2] Again, because these characteristics have been generally discussed in other works, I will only mention them briefly:

---

1. See Cleophus J. LaRue, "Two Ships Passing in the Night," in *What's the Matter with Preaching Today?*, ed. Mike Graves (Louisville, KY: Westminster John Knox Press, 2004), 139–40.

2. Five of these characteristics are listed in *Preaching with Sacred Fire: An Anthology of African American Preaching, 1750 to the Present* (New York: W. W. Norton and Company, 2010), 7–8 and the sixth characteristic was added in the latest edition of *They Like to Never Quit Praisin' God: The Role of Celebration in Preaching* (Cleveland, OH: United Church Press, 2013), 1–4. Also see, "Black Preaching Changed the Course of This Country. What Created That Style?" https://www.washingtonpost.com/news/acts-of-faith/wp/2016/05/09/black-preaching-changed-the-course-of-this-country-what-creates-that-style/.

1. The centrality of the Bible—this is not to be mistaken for a rigid biblical literalism. The Bible is seen as *the* inspired and dynamic source for understanding the world and *the* wise guide for life's decisions. Cleophus J. LaRue suggests: "More than a mere source for texts, in black preaching, the Bible is the single most important source of language, imagery, and story for the sermon."[3]

2. The importance of experiential preaching—the Bible comes alive by means of an eyewitness style of picture painting and narration. The preacher stirs the five senses, and as a result, the hearer does not just hear about John the Baptist in past biblical times; John the Baptist is present in the room, seen, heard, touched, and felt by all. I heard James Forbes Jr. tell the story that Gardner C. Taylor was preaching the biblical story of the prodigal son. In a particularly poignant moment, Forbes recounts that Taylor said, "Look, the boy is coming up the road now!" Forbes says he turned around, looked to the back of the church, and saw the boy coming up the road. The African American sermon is experiential.

3. Existential exegesis—a particular form of exegesis that joins biblical scholarship to existential human need. African American preaching operates from the perspective of a close observation of the Bible and human need, which directs the sermon to resolve existential concern by exegesis of the text. The sermon is never academic alone, but exegesis addresses human need and illustrates for hearers the true meaning of life and living.

4. The inspiration of the Holy Spirit—the preacher is dependent on a power beyond the preacher's power. The Holy Spirit ultimately shapes and delivers the message through the preacher. The sermon is not simply the words of a human being, but the very voice of God speaks through the preacher.

---

3. Cleophus LaRue, *The Heart of Black Preaching* (Louisville, KY: Westminister John Knox Press, 1999), 10.

5. Suspense that leads to celebration—the preacher structures the sermon to hold suspense as long as possible, and after the suspense is resolved, the preacher celebrates the good news with a powerful and uplifting conclusion. The weight that the black church places on a powerful conclusion to a message is unparalleled in any culture. The majority of the time the close is reserved for pure celebration, and close the preacher must.

6. The call and response nature of the sermon—call and response refers to the interaction between preachers and congregations all over black America that allows the audience to partner in shaping and directing the sermon. Based on oral traditions in west and central Africa, the preacher says something and the congregation says something back. The preacher often makes a sermonic plan in the study, but feedback from the audience often leads to improvisations initially unforeseen by the preacher.

7. The performative nature of the sermon—the word of God must be "embodied" in the total person of the preacher, including head (rationality), heart (emotionality), and body (physicality). The word must be incarnated in the total person of the preacher and not just the rational aspects of the preacher's being, hence the sermon, in the best sense of the word, is performed.

With an understanding of characteristics of black preaching, I want to continue to address the question of what black preaching is by looking at Kenyatta Gilbert's discussion of two major scholars in African American preaching, Henry H. Mitchell and Cleophus J. LaRue.

BLACK PREACHING: HENRY H. MITCHELL AND CLEOPHUS J. LARUE

As stated on the Bus Tour, the discipline of African American homiletics in the theological academic community begins with the work of Henry H. Mitchell in the late 1960s and early 1970s. Kenyatta R. Gilbert points out that given the release of Mitchell's work, "few proposals since then have furthered the discussion beyond contrasting [African American preaching] with Eurocentric preaching."[4] Gilbert says, "Given this impasse, the future direction of African American preaching remains indistinct."[5] Gilbert contrasts the scholarship of Henry H. Mitchell and Cleophus J. LaRue as the broad parameters of theoretical discussion within African American homiletics. Gilbert defines Mitchell's work as "rhetorical homiletics" or "rhetorical performative homiletics," and LaRue's work as the "theological-homiletical" or "theological-hermeneutical." What is at stake is a response to the question, what is black preaching?

Gilbert argues that, for Mitchell, the distinguishing mark of black preaching is its rhetorical performative structure, what Mitchell labels, "preaching to the whole person," and what we would identify as joining intellect and emotion in preaching. Mitchell labels preaching to the whole person as "experiential preaching," and marks celebration, particularly in the close of the sermon, as the distinguishing factor of African American preaching. Gilbert points out two critical concerns of the rhetorical performative method of Mitchell. First, it is not always clear that what is being said about God (theology) is at the heart of the creation of the rhetorical experience. Therefore, it is not really clear if the most important thing is the message-bearing task of the preacher (rhetoric), or the word of God (theology).

LaRue would suggest that what makes black preaching distinctive is its hermeneutical lens, that is, the way that African Americans conceive of God and appropriate scripture to their human experience. According to LaRue, the specific distinctiveness of black preaching is (1) the belief in all-powerful God, (2) the sociocultural contextualization of marginalization and oppression, and (3) the black lived experience. Gilbert points out that the critical concern of LaRue's theological-hermeneutical method is that LaRue is not clear how the person of the preacher matters (rhetoric). The most important aspect of the homiletical task is the interpretive

---

4. Kenyatta R. Gilbert, *The Journey and Promise of African American Preaching* (Minneapolis: Fortress Press, 2011), 22.

5. Ibid., 23.

theological task, and the person of message bearer (rhetoric) is not clearly outlined. Gilbert suggests that these two perspectives define the locus of argument within African American homiletics.

I believe that these parameters outlined by Gilbert will and are being influenced by present and soon coming scholarship that includes significant dialogue with other marginalized communities such as Korean and Latino(a), preaching in the African Diaspora, the Global South, and what several young scholars have termed as "communicative expression."[6] These parameters are also being changed by the preaching of African American women and womanists that will even more fully emerge in the fourth era of black preaching. I would also hope that the broader definition of black preaching as inherently rhetorical and theological contained herein would also broaden these parameters.

As an example of the impact of womanist homiletics, in the Bus Tour, we discovered that Donna E. Allen added rhetorical criticism to the study of black preaching as part of constructing a womanist homiletic. While African American scholars such as William H. Pipes, Gerald Lamont Thomas, Isaac Rufus Clark, and others have applied the Aristotelian rhetorical categories of ethos, logos, and pathos to the study of black preaching, Allen's definition and application of rhetorical criticism opens up a new dimension of the study of African American preaching. From the vantage point of the work of Allen, I would like to add more detailed

---

6. In African American cultures, the lines between sacred and secular are often blurred, such that theological ideas find expression found outside the pulpit in and through cultural forms: music, poetry, literature, spoken word, video, art, dance, and others. While this basic phenomenon has always characterized African American life, it is particularly true today, especially among younger generations. At the CTS consultation of African American preaching scholars, younger colleagues drove this point home: authentic black preaching must engage "communicative expression." We must study not only preachers inside the Christian church but also whenever and wherever powerful communicative expression is uttered. Communicative expression encompasses the task of pulpit preaching, but also music, poetry, public discourse, new media, and other cultural forms. Moreover, these younger colleagues pressed the question, "Does black preaching include the preaching of the African diaspora, or are we just limited to these American shores?" See "For Such a Time as This: 2014 Consultation of African American Homileticians," Academy of Preaching and Celebration, Christian Theological Seminary, September 2014, https://cloud.3dissue.com/29434/30219/38984/PS3/index.html?r=25 (accessed February 19, 2016).

rhetorical critical method and analysis, close reading, and ideological criticism.

The addition of close reading to the study of African American preaching allows the discussion of a critical method for studying written sermon texts. Though much of the African American preaching tradition was transmitted orally, there are many written sermonic texts in newspapers, pamphlets, anthologies, books of sermons, sermons published by churches, and the like. There has been little discussion of critical methods of reading in order to interpret individual written sermon texts. I would like to offer close reading as a method to study written sermonic texts of black preaching. As an example, I will present a close reading of Taylor's "His Own Clothes."

The addition of rhetorical criticism to African American preaching again reinforces my argument that African American preaching is inherently theological and rhetorical. Rhetorical criticism allows the discernment of the belief system of the preacher (theology), and how that belief system constitutes an audience (rhetoric). In every sermon, the preacher communicates a belief system, not only verbally, but also nonverbally with gestures, sound, and so forth. When we look through the lens of rhetorical criticism at the belief system (theology), we can notice how the belief system of a specific preacher, in a specific cultural context, forms the audience, and predisposes the audience to act (rhetoric). Preaching is inherently theological and rhetorical. I believe that rhetorical criticism can make a significant contribution to our quest to define the question, what is black preaching? But, first, we must ask, exactly what is rhetorical criticism?

BLACK PREACHING AND RHETORICAL CRITICISM

As discussed on the Bus Tour, Donna E. Allen defines rhetorical criticism as the study of the various persuasive options available to preachers in the creation of their messages and how those options work together to create effects in the preacher and audience.[7] Rhetorical criticism allows

---
7. Allen, *Toward a Womanist Homiletic: Katie Cannon, Alice Walker, and Emancipatory Proclamation*, 8ff.

the critic to see with greater clarity the persuasive choices made by the preacher, and potentially other choices that were not selected. For example, what audience was not mentioned, or, who, in effect, was written out of, or even excluded from the sermon? For Allen, rhetorical criticism is critical in the construction of a womanist homiletic because it can identify "derogatory images of women and patriarchal teachings." Each preacher is making decisive rhetorical choices that include or exclude audiences, and affect the audience's apprehension of the message. Allen believes that knowledge of rhetorical operations on the part of the preacher allows the congregation to respond to and engage the message at the level of "emancipatory praxis."[8] I want to further expand Allen's appropriation of rhetorical criticism for emancipatory praxis by applying the rhetorical method of close reading to "His Own Clothes." First, let me explain what is meant by the use of the term *close reading*.

An important shift occurred in the field of communication and rhetoric in the last thirty years. Though rhetoric was concerned with human speech, until recently, little attention was paid to the study of the inner workings of specific speeches. Critics interested in studying the inner workings of texts sought insights from the field of literary criticism. With the new attention to the inner depths of speeches, a method of "close reading" emerged in rhetorical criticism. According to Michael Leff, one of the leading proponents of close reading, individual and written speech texts have "rhetorical textures," and a certain "integrity and density." Speech texts are not just a compilation of words, sentences, and paragraphs, but rather an organized system of ideas, images, and arguments. *The written text is a world in and of itself and within the boundaries of the text are infinite insights into the mind, heart, and belief system of the speaker and the intended audience.* Close reading allows the critic to peer deeply into the inner world of the speaker, including the speaker's persuasive choices and the speaker's conception of audience.

---

8. The term *emancipatory praxis* is borrowed from Katie Cannon, and Allen defines it as follows: "For Cannon, Alice Walker's creation of the term womanist as a description of what it means to be African American and female is an act of resistance or an emancipatory praxis through language" (Allen, *Toward a Womanist Homiletic: Katie Cannon, Alice Walker, and Emancipatory Proclamation*, 16).

The critique of close reading was that with such close and microscopic analysis of the inner workings of the text, the critic could lose sensitivity to the social and historical dimensions. If there are an infinite number of insights in the text itself, and the text is a world in and of itself, what is the relationship between text and context? How does context influence the inner workings of the text? The concept of "intertextuality" emerged as the view that texts cannot be conceived or understood in isolation in and of themselves, but only in relation to other texts and utterances. By adding intertextuality to close reading, one captures the context, the historical and social dimensions of the text. The critic can chart how the speaker borrows different voices and language from other texts, "orchestrating" them into a rhetorical performance. An example of this form of critical close reading is John M. Murphy's study of President Bill Clinton's November 1993 address in Memphis, Tennessee, to a meeting of African American clergy.[9] Murphy recognized Clinton's ability to borrow the voice and language of the African American homiletic tradition, specifically one of its chief practitioners, Martin Luther King Jr., and join it with the voice and language of the liberal tradition of American politics. Clinton orchestrated both of these traditions into a remarkable rhetorical performance for the assembled audience of African American preachers.

Beyond intertextuality, rhetorical scholars continued to ask: When considering the context of the text, what might we be specifically looking for? One response is that the critic might look for ideological dimensions of the text, hence ideological criticism arose. While the term *ideology* is used in many different contexts, let me be very specific. Anthony Giddens defines ideology as beliefs within "modes of lived existence."[10] Ideologies are communicated belief systems (i.e., words, pictures, texts, sounds, and so forth) that impact and define an artifact of communication (i.e., sermon text) and the attempt to influence behavior within a cultural context. It is virtually impossible to have discourse and not have ideology. Ideology is connected to myths, as Georges Sorel writes: "Myths are not descriptions

---

9. John M. Murphy, "Inventing Authority: Bill Clinton, Martin Luther King, Jr., and the Orchestration of Rhetorical Traditions," *Quarterly Journal of Speech* 83 (1997): 71–89.

10. Anthony Giddens, *Central Problems in Social Theory* (Berkley and Los Angeles: University of California Press, 1979), 183.

of things, but expressions of a determination to act. . . . A myth . . . is, at bottom, identical with the convictions of a group, being the expression of those convictions in the language of movement."[11]

In pure rhetorical terms, theology is a form of ideology, and I will begin to use ideology/theology interchangeably. Again, my suggestion is not to demean or denigrate theology by calling it ideology, but simply to make the point that theology is a communicated belief system seeking to influence behavior in a cultural context. The main proponent of ideological criticism is Michael Calvin McGhee.[12]

As a precursor to understanding McGhee, it is important to discuss Maurice Charland.[13] Charland argues that not only does ideology/theology seek to influence behavior, but it also constitutes and calls the audience itself into being. The audience is formed by responses to ideological/theological claims of the preacher. According to Charland, the preacher constitutes or calls "the people" into being.

As an example of Charland's thinking, I have heard countless American politicians claim to be speaking for the "American people." No matter a politician's position on an issue or legislative concern, over and over again the consistent refrain is: "The American people want [or do not want] . . ." or "I am speaking or voting on behalf of the American people." When these statements are critically examined, the rhetorical critic asks, "Who are the American people the speaker is referring to?" Often, the speaker is referring to a slice of the American public who agrees with their ideology, or, in Charland's terms, the part of the audience formed by the speaker's ideology. Speakers buttress their arguments by invoking what

---

11. Michael Calvin McGee, "In Search of 'the People': A Rhetorical Alternative," in *Contemporary Rhetorical Theory*, ed. John Louis Lucaites, Celeste Michelle Condit, Sally Caudill (New York: The Guilford Press, 1999), 346.

12. Michael Calvin McGee theorizes that condensed forms of "ideology" known as "ideographs" operate in public communication as instruments of political consciousness. Ideographs are the building blocks of ideology, and for McGee, ideology is political language composed of slogan-like terms signifying collective commitment (i.e., freedom, equality, justice). See Michael Calvin McGee, "The 'Ideograph': A Link between Rhetoric and Ideology," in *Readings in Rhetorical Criticism*, ed. Carl R. Burgchardt, 3rd ed. (Pennsylvania: Strata Publishing, 2005), 451. Maurice Charland, "Constitutive Rhetoric: The Case of the Peuple Quebocois," *Quarterly Journal of Speech* 73 (1987): 133–50.

13. Charland, "Constitutive Rhetoric: The Case of the Peuple Quebecois."

is, in essence, rhetorical fiction. In terms of the speaker's argument, there are no American people, except the one constructed by the speaker, who claims to be speaking for the American people.

McGee concurs with Charland and defines "the people" as a linguistic phenomena introduced into public arguments by the speaker to legitimize arguments. For McGee, consistent rhetorical appeals to "the people" is "argumentative gymnastics," "by definition an argumentative fallacy," and hence an "irrational form of persuasion." McGee identifies this argumentative gymnastics by its Latin name, *argumentum ad populam*.[14]

For McGee, in purely objective terms, "the only human reality is that of the individual; groups, whether as small as a Sunday-school class or as big as a whole society, are infused with an artificial identity."[15] This means that the human socialization process is the intensive and continual exercise in persuading an individual to give up individual identity to form with a group, and as McGee says, "not only when mothers attempt to housebreak them, but also later in life when governors ask them to obey a law or to die in war for God and country."[16] The people are more *process* than *phenomenon*. The people as an essential rhetorical fiction are both a "social" and "objective" reality, both real and fictitious at the same time. The speaker constructs "the people," and when the people are constructed by the speaker, "the people" often act in reality.

McGee quotes Hitler to describe the rhetorical process by which a leader transforms individuals into "the people":

> By "people" I mean all those hundreds of thousands who fundamentally long for the same thing without finding the words in detail to describe the outward appearance of what is before the inner eye. For with all great reforms the remarkable thing is that at first they have as their champion only a single individual, but as their supporters many millions. For centuries their goal is often the inner ardent wish of hundreds of thousands, till one man stands up as the proclaimer of such a general

---

14. Michael Calvin McGee, "In Search of 'the People': A Rhetorical Alternative," in *Contemporary Rhetorical Theory: A Reader*, ed. John Louis Lucaites, Celeste Michelle Condit, Sally Caudill (New York: Guilford Press, 1999), 341.

15. Ibid., 345.

16. Ibid.

will and as the flag-bearer of an old longing he helps it to victory in the form of a new idea.[17]

Hitler suggests that individuals have a "predisposition" toward a particular expression of the popular will, but are unaware of it. Their identity as a "people" is contained in maxims and national ideological commitments that remain "inner ardent wishes." Because basically they are individuals who long for the same thing, there is no such thing as a people, and they have no collective identity to achieve collective unity and goals because they cannot describe what is before their "inner eye." The duty of the champion, advocate, charismatic leader, and in this instance, the preacher, is to find cultural language and memory, an "old longing" (might be centuries old), in McGee's terms, and "help it to victory." The preacher is a "flag-bearer" for the old longing, and by transforming such longings into a new idea, the preacher forms the people. By forming the people, the preacher actualizes the audience's predisposition to act, thus creating a united "people" whose collective power will warrant any "reform" against any other power on earth. It is through cultural language and memory that the being of a historical people is made concrete in the world.

For McGee, the political or theological language of a people is a "felt quality of life." A rhetorical opportunity occurs to form "the people" when a "felt quality" of life encounters a countervailing and hostile felt quality, the forces of delegitimization of cultural memory and language. At this point, radical reflection occurs, the preacher names the deep longing or felt quality, and the consciousness of a people emerge in the preacher's language. Developing a concept from Walter Benjamin, McGee explains how radical reflection occurs: "In a present moment of danger an individual (or an individual speaking on behalf of a people) reaches into the magazine of cultural memory and brings forward a fragment of the past around which to crystallize resistance to a present danger."[18]

---

17. Ibid., 344.

18. John Angus Campbell, "Between the Fragment and the Icon: Prospect for a Rhetorical House on the Middle Way," *Western Journal of Speech Communication* 54 (Summer, 1990): 351.

The reality of "the people" is a constructed and mythical rhetorical creation. The proclaimer presents a description of reality that amounts to ideology, political or theological. If "the people" accept the ideology, then the speaker becomes the leader. The new leader is a kind of rhetorical fiction created by "the people" in response to the affirmation of cultural memory. I want now to look at a rhetorical analysis of Gardner C. Taylor's sermon "His Own Clothes," and how through the use of deep longings and cultural memory, Taylor forms a victorious Christian people.

Close Reading of "His Own Clothes"

Before we begin rhetorical analysis, there are a few comments that are important to make. First, within rhetorical critical circles, it is of first importance to establish the viability of the text. Gardner C. Taylor preached "His Own Clothes" on several occasions and in numerous places, with at least two versions of the sermon published.[19] Because oral sermonic presentations are never exactly the same, written texts may vary in wording, phrasing, and illustrations, though the ultimate content of the sermons is relatively the same.[20] The version of the sermon that I chose for this analysis is found in *The Words of Gardner Calvin Taylor*, vol. 3, *Quintessential Classics, 1980–Present*.[21] Second, so as to not interrupt the flow of rhetorical analysis, I will not spend time on Taylor's biography. For those who are not familiar with Taylor, there are many available sources that will help with his biography. Third, there are voluminous discussions of Taylor's significance and meaning for all of preaching, his residence within the African American preaching tradition, and his evidence of the characteristics of black preaching, such as we discussed in the opening section of this chapter. These deliberations would include Taylor's oratorical style,

---

19. See Simmons and Thomas, *Preaching with Sacred Fire: An Anthology of African American Preaching, 1750 to the Present*, 834–40.

20. An audio version of "His Own Clothes" is found on disc 1 of *Essential Taylor CD* (Valley Forge, PA: Judson Press, 2001).

21. Though the version of the sermon "His Own Clothes" is found in Gardner C. Taylor, *The Words of Gardner C. Taylor*, vol. 3, *Quintessential Classics 1980–Present*, compiled by Edward L. Taylor (Valley Forge, PA: Judson Press, 2000), 116–21, the reader would do well to take notice of the entire series, The Words of Gardner Taylor, vols. 1-6, compiled by Edward L. Taylor (Valley Forge, PA: Judson Press, 2004).

sermon preparation process, view of scripture, sermon sources, prophetic preaching, poetic persuasion, theology, formation of moral community, crossover preaching, and much more. The reader can find these discussions readily available. Therefore, I will limit my comments of these matters.[22] Fourth, Taylor, like Samuel DeWitt Proctor, was hesitant to limit his preaching by the label "black preaching," even as he was popularly called "the Dean of Black Preaching." He was in the strand whose preaching was African American through and through, though he felt it was important to stress the commonality with all preaching rather than the distinctives of black preaching. Finally, Taylor is illustrative of the fact that African American preaching, in its appeal to all human beings, calls forth the deep longing for freedom, dignity, liberation, and belonging to the human family in individuals, and connects it with those same longings in the gospel of Jesus Christ, such that when the preacher champions the gospel of Jesus Christ to victory, a victorious Christian people are formed and ready to act. This rhetorical analysis of "His Own Clothes" will illustrate that Gardner C. Taylor is a preacher, poet, prophet, conjurer, shaman, griot, sermonic playwright, and storyteller. Taylor champions and connects the deep longings of the Christian tradition with the longings of African Americans, and forms the audience into "a people," a victorious Christian army.

Taylor begins the sermon forming the hearers into a Christian people by his first statement that announces the theme of the sermon: "Short of the cross itself and the betrayal by Judas, what the soldiers did to Jesus may have well been the most humiliating part of our Lord's suffering for

---

22. Gerald Lemont Thomas, *African American Preaching: The Contribution of Dr. Gardner C. Taylor* (New York: Peter Lang, 2004); *Our Sufficiency Is of God*, ed. Timothy George, James Earl Massey, and Robert Smith Jr. (Macon, GA: Mercer University Press, 2010), *Gardner C. Taylor: Submissions to the Dean*, ed. J. Doulas Wiley and Ivan Douglass Hicks (Chicago: Urban Ministries, Inc., 2009). Jerry M. Carter Jr., "The Audible Sacrament: The Sacramentality of Gardner C. Taylor's Preaching" (PhD diss., Drew University, 2009), http://gradworks.umi.com/32/94/3294227.html. Susan Bond, "To Hear the Angel's Wings: Apocalyptic Language and the Formation of Moral Community with Reference to the Sermons of Gardner C. Taylor" (PhD diss., Vanderbilt University, 1996). Taylor published his 1975–76 Lyman Beecher Lectures in *How Shall They Preach* (Elgin, IL: Progressive Baptist Publishing House, 1977). Jared E. Alcantara, *Crossover Preaching: Intercultural-Improvisational Homiletics with Gardner C. Taylor* (Downers Grove, IL: IVP Academic, 2015).

you and me" (see Appendix A, p. 185, lines 4–5). Here, in the opening sentence, we find the first and ultimate Christian memory that he is going to champion to victory: Jesus and his suffering redemption. He surfaces ancient Christian doctrine: Christ suffered to redeem the world. Then to ensure that it does not remain as an abstract intellectual concept, he says, "for you and me." Christ suffered to redeem the world, and the phrase "for you and me" makes it intensely personal, a matter of the individual longing in the human heart for redemption from the devastation of sin and brokenness. As a matter of fact, he is going to come back to this theme over and over again. Jerry M. Carter convincingly argues that one of the great characteristics of Taylor's preaching is its emphasis on the redemptive Christ event of scripture.[23] Carter suggests the redemptive Christ is Taylor's main ideological/theological belief, and as a result, the anchor of Taylor's preaching. As a testament to Carter's assertion, in this sermon, including the aforementioned, "the most humiliating part of our Lord's suffering and death for you and me" (line 5), Taylor mentions the redemptive death of Jesus at least sixteen times:

> "ridicule the soldiers heaped upon our Lord on the night leading to his crucifixion" (line 20–21)

> "the Son of God, the Savior of the world, the blessed Redeemer, being the object or the rude jokes" (lines 23–24)

> "his death on our behalf" (line 26)

> "Through all of these things Jesus passed in the interest of all of our souls" (37–38)

> "glib dismissal of the church for which Christ died" (75)

> "love for the Lord who has done so much for us" (79–80)

---

23. For a thorough analysis of the christocentric redemptive nature of Taylor's preaching, see Carter, "The Audible Sacrament: The Sacramentality of Gardner C. Taylor's Preaching," 89ff. Carter says, "There is nothing more central to Christian preaching than the Christ event (redemptive suffering) for Gardner Taylor. . . The Christ event is the normative lens through which Taylor views all of Scripture."

"Have I cloaked the savior of the world . . . ?" (97)

"making sport of the Son of God" (102)

"they put on our Lord his own clothes" (103)

"Jesus in his own clothes going to Calvary" (116)

"In his own clothes, he went to Calvary" (123)

"On no other day did Jesus have to go back to finish his work at Calvary" (124–125)

"He appeared to put away sin at the sacrifice of himself" (126)

"So Christ was once offered to bear the sins of many" (126–27)

"He died in his own clothes as Savior and Redeemer" (127–28)

The redemptive work of the Christ is the major longing in the Christian heart that he drives to victory and forms a redeemed and victorious Christian audience.

Taylor drives home the meaning of Christ's redemptive suffering by linking the suffering of Christ to the human longing for dignity worthy of belonging to the human family (4–7). What would take away one's human dignity and attempt to cast one as outside the human family? Suffering yes, but a particular kind of suffering. Suffering that attempts to mock the person as a human being. Taylor says, "There is something uniquely cruel in being laughed at, mocked, set apart from one's fellows and made the target of ugly jibes, cruel comments, and cutting laughter" (10–11).

Taylor then drops deep into the cultural memory of the African American experience of being ridiculed in America. He shapes the Christian message to a particular African American historical experience representing the felt quality of life and begins to form the audience. He connects Jesus's experience of being ridiculed as the Savior of the world to the black experience of being ridiculed:

One of the most painful and sinister weapons used historically against black people in this country was mockery and ridicule. Physical features were caricatured and exaggerated, and so the large white-lipped, wide-eyed, blackened face in minstrel shows became the notion of the way black people looked and acted. . . . The purpose of the foot-shuffling, head-scratching, wide-grinning, ghost frightened darky, was to ridicule, scorn, and humiliate. (11–17)

But, the main purpose of the sermon is not the suffering of black people, so he quickly turns the camera lens of our attention back to Jesus by the statement, "Far crueler than our own (black) experience of scorn was the kind of ridicule that the soldiers heaped upon our Lord on the night heading to his crucifixion" (20–21). For poetic emphasis, he says that "it chills the spirit to think of the Son of God, the Savior of the world, the blessed Redeemer being the object of rude jokes, and the broad barracks humor of these rough and dull-witted soldiers" (23–25).

He then takes us through the crucifixion by describing the Roman ritual of condemnation and gives us the details of Jesus moving toward his death as he reminds us again that he did it for us. He describes the Lord's agony in Gethsemane, the betrayal, the chains—and they blindfolded "our Lord" and struck him, slapping him in the face and taunting him (28–29). Following all of this, they scourged him on the platform where the trial had been and in the sight of all. Taylor spares not the details of the brutal act:

> The victim was stripped down to the waist and was stretched against a pillar with hands tied. The instrument of torture was a long leather strip, studded with pieces of lead and bits of bone. The whip left lashes, and the lead and bone tore out chunks of flesh. Some died under the lash, and others emerged from the torture raving mad. . . . All of these things Jesus went through "in the interest of all of our souls." (33–38)

After the vivid and emotionally gripping description of scourging, notice the refrain at the end: Jesus went through all of this in the interest of "our" souls. Taylor never allows the redemptive work of Christ to remain abstract; it is always intimate and personal. He reminds us that all of this was only preliminary and secondary to the supreme sacrifice of Calvary.

CHAPTER THREE

After Jesus was whipped, then sentence was pronounced, "death by crucifixion." The condemned was "lifted on a cross, slowly died, and left that the vultures and carrion crows might dispose of the body" (44–45).

After sentencing, soldiers were told to go and prepare the cross, and "Jesus our Lord" was turned over to the personal guards of Pontius Pilate as governor. Taylor describes these men as

> hard-bitten professional soldiers who chafed at their unpleasant assignment in such a hot, fly-ridden place as Palestine and all these strange and offensive people.... One of their pleasures was to taunt and torture convicted criminals who cringed before them like cornered and helpless animals. The Son of God was turned over to them, and they went to work with their cruel jibes. (50–55)

They stripped him of *his own clothes*. Having heard rumors of the charge that he claimed to be a king:

> They jammed a reed in his hand to mock, a scepter, and plaited a crown made of thorn bush for his brow, and flung around the Lord's shoulder an old faded red tunic.... All this was done to mock him as king, and so they bowed down in ridicule as if to honor and worship him ... then their loud, uncouth laughter rang and echoed through the barracks. (58–64)

Taylor then draws a comparison between those who mocked the Lord in the text and those who mock the Lord still today. He starts outside the church with those who mock and dispute Jesus as Savior of the world. They respect and honor Jesus and say, "His ethics are splendid principle of conduct and human relations.... As for his church, 'It's all right for those who need it, but I do not go to church. I do not feel need of it, really'" (71–72). He then moves inside the church to those who put garments of mock loyalty on the Lord and call his name, but feel no deep loyalty. He then indicts the American nation as godless. Finally, he turns to himself and the believer and asks, "Have I put fake garment on the Lord Jesus? Have I cloaked the Savior of the world in scarlet robes of pretense?" (97–98). Again, the goal is to ensure that the words do not remain abstract, but are intensely personal.

After challenging those outside the church, those inside the church, the nation, and the believer, he goes back to the soldiers. When they tired of their sport, they took the fake clothes off him and put *his own clothes* back on him as final preparation for crucifixion. He does not describe the crucifixion with the relentless details of the mockery and ridicule as he did the whipping of Jesus. He ends the scene with Jesus heading out to be crucified because he has already mentioned that the condemned died slowly and the body was left for vultures and crows to dispose of.

He now moves to resolve the tension of the ridicule and the crucifixion. He tells the audience what it all means. He says, *his own clothes* say worlds to us (104). He paints the picture that we need to see Jesus "as he is," and "not mocked and ridiculed by false respect and pious hypocrisy" (104–5). He begins to champion Jesus to victory and what it means practically for the hearer's life. When the hearer sees Jesus in his own clothes, representative of "his true character and force," the hearer cries out for forgiveness, approval, and good favor (106). According to Taylor, when the hearer sees Jesus as he is, it helps us see ourselves as we are and be encouraged to do better (109). The hearer must examine him- or herself and ask the question: "Did I do my best?"

Taylor provides the illustration of Edmund Spencer, a student who pulled seventeen drowning people out of Lake Michigan. When they dragged him out of the water and carried him to his dorm room, he asked in his exhaustion, "Did I do my best?" (109–13). Taylor, following Spencer, challenges himself every time he preaches by asking, "Did I do my best?" He challenges the officers, choir members, ushers of the church by asking, "Did you do your best?" (115). Taylor encourages us to do our best by saying that "Jesus in *his own clothes* going up to Calvary did his best" (116).

He turns now to the details of the victory by the use of allegory. He connects the crucifixion of Jesus to the victory recorded in the Hebrew prophet Isaiah of the one who is victorious with dyed and stained garments (Isa 63). He says that Jesus's garments, going up the lonely hill of Calvary, were rolled in blood, making understandable the old cry of Isaiah (the deep longing of Hebrew prophets):

CHAPTER THREE

"Who is this that cometh out of Edom? With dyed clothes from Bosrah? this that is glorious in his apparel, travelling in the greatness of his strength?" (Isaiah 63:1). We ask, "Wherefore art thou red in thine apparel, and thy garments like him that treadeth in the winefat?" (v. 2). And he answers "I have trodden the winepress alone . . . for the day of vengeance is in mine heart, and the year of my redeemed is come" (vv. 3-4). (116–22)

By the use of allegory, Taylor connects Jesus with the one coming out of Edom with dyed garments and announces the day of vengeance of God and the year of the redeemed is come. Jesus has now ridden to victory and the day of the redeemed, that is, those who have been mocked and ridiculed, their day of victory has come. Those who have been cast from the human family are human family members once again—the day of victory has come.

Now, Taylor gives the formal announcement of the good news of the victory such that celebration can begin. Taylor says, "In *his own clothes* he went to Calvary, and made everything alright, not temporarily all right but now for always" (123–24). This is the language and mood of celebration and victory that is a characteristic of African American preaching that we referred to in the opening section of this chapter. He joyously and ecstatically reinforces the victory: "At Calvary Christ was at his best. Nothing had been left undone. On no other day does Jesus have to go back. . . . He died in his own clothes as Savior and Redeemer. Once for all. It is all right now" (124–28). Taylor goes back to Isaiah to reinforce the victory: "It is all right now. The crooked way has been made straight (Isa 40:1). We may arise now and shine for the light has come (Isa 60:1). It is all right now" (128–29).

The final image of victory and celebration is the second coming of Jesus Christ. Along with Taylor's belief in redemptive suffering is his belief in the second coming of Jesus.[24] Taylor shifts the hearers to the joy of eschatological coming of Christ by hinting in one line in the midst of victory and celebration, "We shall see him yet in other clothes" (180). Taylor alludes to Ellen White, the prophetess of Seventh Day Adventism:

---

24. For discussion of Taylor's eschatological emphasis in preaching, see Jerry Carter, "The Audible Sacrament: The Sacramentality of Gardner C. Taylor's Preaching," 80.

> She pictures that day when Christ shall appear with no longer an old, faded red cloak around his shoulders, no longer mocked by soldiers, no longer wearing the simple garments of this earth. Every eye shall see him. We shall see him as heaven's king, victor over death, hell, and the grave, admired of angels. Every eye shall see him. Ten thousand time ten thousands and thousands upon thousands of angels and the triumphant sons and daughters of God up ten thousands will escort him. On his vesture, his clothes, shall be written King of King and Lord of Lords. (130–37)

The process is complete now; the people are formed, a victorious African American Christian people. The people are not mocked, ridiculed, or laughed at. The people are victorious in Jesus Christ, and ready to act out their victory in the world.

Now, let me offer a few concluding observations. Besides the formation of Christian community based upon championing the redemptive Christ to victory, there are several other longings that Taylor advocated in forming African Americans into "the people." First, he calls to the deep longing for freedom and dignity in the black experience. The black experience in America of being marginalized, mocked, and ridiculed facilitated an ease of identification with a crucified Savior of the Bible who was mocked and ridiculed. And when the crucified Savior of the world was victorious, black people who believed in the Savior were victorious and triumphant as well. This is the most obvious explanation as to why historically the African American church has often been so christocentric. Taylor calls forth this deep longing, and in the best homiletical and celebrative practices of the African American preaching tradition, helps the longing to victory.

It is not accidental that Taylor gives great specificity to the details of Jesus being whipped, and the illusion to crows eating the flesh of the dead after they have been crucified. The rhetorical choice of these descriptive details is to reach into the magazine of cultural memory and encounter forces hostile to the felt quality of African American life. Radical reflection occurs and the consciousness of a people emerges in the cultural memory of the preacher's language. The impacts of the details to cultural memory of Jesus being whipped to African Americans being whipped are so obvious that I would hope it needs no further comment or explanation.

Less obvious would be the allusion to the crows eating the flesh of the crucified dead. This is an allusion to lynching, and lynching is the most visible and painful symbol in black cultural memory of the hostility to black life and humanity. Billie Holiday sang a protest song, "Strange Fruit,"[25] that *Time* magazine labeled as the "song of the century." The song draws the stark conclusion that black bodies lynched are "strange fruit" hanging from Southern trees, what she calls "a strange and bitter crop."

As soon as lynching became the violent tactic of choice to murder, dehumanize, and intimidate black people, African Americans established the connection that lynching was a form of crucifixion and crucifixion was a form of lynching. James Cone, in his marvelous book *The Cross and the Lynching Tree*, gives theological explanation to this belief in the souls of black people:

> African Americans embraced the story of Jesus, the crucified Christ, whose death they claimed paradoxically gave them life, just as God resurrected him in the life of the earliest Christian community. While the lynching tree symbolized white power and "black death," the cross symbolized divine power and "black life"—God overcoming the power of sin and death.[26]

Taylor made intentional rhetorical choices with the details of the language of Jesus being whipped and crows eating the bodies of the crucified dead to form African Americans into "a people."

The question must be asked: Does one have to be an African American to be formed as part of Taylor's "the people"? Another way to ask this same question is this: Would only African Americans have an appreciation of Taylor's sermon? People of all races and nations and peoples have found

---

25. On August 7, 1930, two African American teenagers, Thomas Shipp and Abram Smith, were lynched by a violent mob in Marion, Indiana. Years later, moved by the infamous photograph taken that night, Abel Meeropol, a Jewish high school teacher in New York City, wrote a protest song entitled "Strange Fruit." The song soon became a signature of a young jazz singer named Billie Holiday, the unforgettable finale of her live performances.

26. James H. Cone, *The Cross and the Lynching Tree* (Maryknoll, NY: Orbis Books), 18.

"It's Alright Now"

Taylor's preaching an encouragement and a place of spiritual uplift. Taylor has received voluminous awards and commendations, even being cited as one of the twelve greatest preachers in the English-speaking world. In this sermon, through the particularity of the African American experience of the exclusion of freedom, Taylor speaks to the universal longing and struggle for freedom that is in every person. Mocking and ridicule to exclude people from the human family is universal. One does not have to be African American to have had this part of the black experience. The universality of the African American experience speaks to people who are not African American, but instead, based upon similarity of experience, have become part of "the people."

Earlier, and we saw this in the last paragraph, we said that rhetorical criticism allows the critic to look closely at the persuasive choices of the speaker. Taylor made definitive rhetorical choices that both *included* and *excluded* material in order to speak to the deep longings in "the people." Taylor, for example, excludes any language that specifically refers to the particularity of the perpetrators of the ridicule and mockery of black people. By alluding to the particularity of the Roman Praetorian Guard, he is connecting to the cultural memory of the whipping and lynching of black people, but he does not mention race, skin color, ethnicity, or heritage of the American perpetrators. He does not single out Klan members, White Citizens Councils, sheriffs, or the Constitution itself, which defined blacks as three-fifths of a person. His language makes it a sin problem. The listeners know the perpetrators, and there is no need to shame, induce guilt, or mock and ridicule anyone. Each listener is free to choose their response to the cultural memory that is not only in African American people, but also in the "American people" as to the treatment of black people. Taylor offers redemption and healing to "the people" who perpetrated crimes against black people. Taylor offers the victory of the gospel of Jesus Christ both to the perpetrators as well to those upon whom the mockery and ridicule were visited. Taylor includes everyone who wants to be included in "the people."

Finally, I want to speak to the phrase "It's all right now." This phrase is so important that I put it in the title as the summary statement to the entire process of forming a victorious Christian army. This phrase has been deep in the cultural memory and magazine of African American people for centuries. In the secular music of black culture—jazz, blues, rhythm and blues, hip-hop—you will find some version of "it's all right now," "it's gonna be all right," or "it's all right." In music written and inspired by the black religious experience, the negro spirituals, quartet music, gospel music, praise and worship, and any other classification of inspirational music, you will find the phrase "It's all right now." The phrase has always had the connotation of comfort after a significantly rigorous battle or challenge. The fight was hard and the struggle gut-wrenching, but the victory has been won and it's all right now. The gospel group Alvin Darling & Celebration gives an example to help us understand the meaning of this phrase. In their song "It's All Right Now," Alvin Darling gives testimony that his child was sick and Jesus stepped in and "It's all right now." Following Darling, one singer gives her testimony and sings about her sister who was sick and suffering deeply with sickness. She recounts that her sister died and went to be home with the Lord and because of 2 Corinthians 5:8, where Paul says to be absent from the body is to be present with the Lord, she sings: "no more sorrow—no more tears—waited for a long time—I waited for a mighty long time, but it is all right now."[27]

When I was the pastor of a congregation, a young man was seriously sick from an AIDS-related illness. The illness ravaged the body of this young man and he was near death. I shall never forget the mother who got in bed with her child, took the young man in her arms, and sang, "It is all right now." The mother signifies that they have come through the worst, and something brighter is up ahead beyond death. Taylor, in the concluding celebration, figuratively as a father, based upon the redemptive victory of the Savior of the world, takes "the people" in his arms, and says, "It is all right now." The battle has been fought and the victory has been won, brighter days are ahead. Taylor channels the eschatological hope in Isaiah—"Once for all. It is all right now. It is all right now. The crooked way has been made straight; we may arise and shine for our light has come"

---

27. "It's All Right Now," Alvin Darling & Celebration, www.youtube.com/watch?v=27fHyGrwZOg.

(128–129). This phrase is eschatological hope as declarative witness. This hope in Christ sustained and made sense of the evil, dehumanization, vicious violence, and outright hate, and allowed "a people," excluded from the human community, to experience themselves as victorious, and live a life as a full human being despite the odds and the forces arrayed against them. The preacher reminded the people, "It's all right now."

I started out this chapter by suggesting that I would do a close reading of Gardner C. Taylor's sermon "His Own Clothes" and offer some insight as to what black preaching is. In the spirit of honest disclosure, the reader has discovered that a definitive definition of black preaching escapes us once again. While we look for the definitive definition, every generation must make its contribution to define this elusive yet potent and powerful tradition of black preaching. This chapter is simply what one student of black preaching wanted to add to the conversation. Though not clearly able to define what black preaching is, the reader will be able to clearly see how African American preaching functions in Taylor's sermon "His Own Clothes": black preaching calls forth the deep longing for liberation, ultimately for belonging to the human family, in individuals, and connects it with those same longings in the gospel of Jesus Christ, such that when the preacher champions the gospel to victory, a victorious people are formed and ready to act.

Chapter Four
"Keepin' It Real":
The Validity of the Existentially Authentic Performance

In response to Henry H. Mitchell's chapter in *The Renewed Homiletic*, entitled "Celebration Renewed," Valerie Bridgeman comments that the "next, natural step" beyond Mitchell's groundbreaking work in preaching is the "poetic sermonic form."[1] *The Renewed Homiletic* revisits the aforementioned paradigm shift in preaching that occurred when Charles Rice, Fred Craddock, David Buttrick, Eugene Lowry, and Henry H. Mitchell reshaped Euro-American preaching with inductive, narrative, and experiential approaches to preaching. Bridgeman's comment is meant to suggest that just as this movement forty years ago revolutionized preaching, the next movement will be the sermon crafted as a poem. She goes further in her response to give more definition to her claim, and even gives an example of a poetic sermon.

In a conversation with Bridgeman about her response to Mitchell, she indicated that there is now a generation that has been raised with hip-hop music, spoken word, poetry slams, and now Gospel Slam.[2] This generation finds the poetic a natural form of speech in proclamation. Her concern was that that they would come to believe that there is no place in

---

1. O. Wesley Allen, Jr., ed. *The Renewed Homiletic*, "Celebration Renewed" (Minneapolis, MN: Fortress Press, 2007), 63–80.

2. Gospel Slam is an event, modeled after the famous poetry slams and incorporating elements of the Moth story hour, during which young adults perform their original three-minute interpretations of the theme at the Academy of Preachers in any spoken form: poetry, rap, testimony, story, homily, parable, even comedy. See www.academyofpreachers.net/gospel-slam/ and www.gospelslam.net.

the church for their poetic form of proclamation. She said the church is put off by the profane language and does not realize how sacred this generation believes life is, despite the vulgar ways they talk about it. They use vulgarity to make a sacred point. Several years ago, a twenty-six-year-old pastor was fired for attending rapper Rick Ross's concert. Deacon Miles Langley of Mt. Salem Baptist Church of North Carolina said that they knew there would be mixed opinions in regard to their action. He explained the decision in this manner: "This is not how we do things here at Mt. Salem. We cannot have a pastor praising the world one minute then praising the Lord the next. Period."[3] In *The Renewed Homiletic*, Bridgeman provocatively calls vulgar sacred language "holy profanity."[4]

Holy profanity is indicative of the fact that in African American culture, the lines between sacred and secular are often blurred, such that speech about God occurs in many religious and cultural forms and practices. At the April 2014 consultation of African American homileticians, several younger scholars drove home the point that authentic black preaching must engage "communicative expression." Communicative expression encompasses the study of the black preaching through the examination of black sacred rhetoric, inclusive of music, poetry, public discourse, new media, and other cultural forms. The study of communicative expression allows examination of the preaching of, for example, non-Christian preachers such as Nation of Islam minister Louis Farrakhan, preaching in the African Diaspora, and also practitioners of hip-hop poetics.

Bridgeman's assessment of the potential of the poetic form in contemporary preaching opens the possibility that homileticians can learn lessons from the varied forms of black sacred rhetoric for more effective preaching. Taking her claim seriously, I will take a brief look at what lessons preaching can glean from the poetic generation by examining the poetry of Jay-Z, a critically acclaimed representative of contemporary poetry in hip-hop music. Specifically, I will consider the question, what might preachers learn from the distinctiveness of the best of hip-hop communi-

---

3. See Cherese Jackson, "North Carolina Pastor Fired for Attending Rick Ross Concert," *Liberty Voice*, Aug. 6, 2013, http://guardianlv.com/2013/08/north-carolina-pastor-for-attending-rick-ross-concert/ (accessed August 19, 2013).

4. Ibid., 75.

cation about excellence in preaching? I will position Jay-Z as a rhetorical critic, and discuss what he considers excellence in hip-hop communication under the rubric of "the real" and "the validity of the existential authentic performance." I want to start by looking at the dominant cultural reality of hip-hop, "the real."[5]

JAY-Z AND CRITERIA FOR THE REAL

Thomas H. Kane, in an article entitled "Bringing the Real: Lacan and Tupac," connects Tupac Shakur and the hip-hop term "the real" with post-structuralist theorist Jacques Lacan's concept of "the Real."[6] Kane argues that the dominant cultural logic in hip-hop is the real, and what is meant is an *existentially authentic performance*.[7] Kane goes to great lengths to argue that when Tupac Shakur says that he is "bringing the real," he is making several claims on several levels, and the one that is most significant for this chapter is that Tupac is "claiming in his performance and in his *being*—he is racially representative, or as the title of one of his early tunes admonishes, that he's strictly representin."[8] For Tupac, the real is to close the gap between representation in words and song and the actual day-to-day reality that one is living. To be real is to rap about a reality and live the reality that one is rapping about. For Tupac, it is difficult to accept rappers who rap about the reality of the ghetto life and then appear on the American Music Awards in suits and ties as being real. To be real is to rap about the violence and rage in the ghetto because one lives the violence and rage in the ghetto. Kane does an extensive analysis of Tupac Shakur's concept of the real, much of which, though very interesting, is beyond the scope of this chapter.

---

5. My goal is not to glorify and over-romanticize an uncritical hip-hop genre and suggest that all of the music and poetry is acceptable, given often misogynistic, violent, derogatory, homophobic, and materialistic lyrics and images. On the other hand, this also does not mean that the entire genre of hip-hop is to be summarily rejected and demonized without consideration of the artist, message, mood, form, and content.

6. Thomas Kane, "Bringing the Real: Lacan and Tupac," in *Prospects: An Annual of American Cultural Studies* 27 (2002): 641–63.

7. Ibid., 642.

8. Ibid.

Jay-Z also discusses the importance of the real to hip-hop. He acknowledges that even though the term "keeping it real" has been overused and has almost become meaningless, realness is essential. He contends that the greatness of hip-hop is that it keeps it real and when hip-hop begins to substitute "style for substance" and loses its "signature and vitality," then hip-hop will go the diminished way of other dormant musical genres, such as disco and the blues.[9]

While many people would not think of Jay-Z as a rhetorical critic, I find that is exactly what he is when he offers criteria and commentary by which we can know the real:

> The realness comes from how an MC shapes whatever their experience into a rhyme. It is in the logic the lyrics follow, the emotional truth that supports it, the human motivations the MC fills in, and the commitment to getting even the smallest details right. That's probably true for all stories, whether they're in book or movies or songs.[10] [I add sermons to this list.]

He then mentions the movie *Menace II Society* as a film that was real.[11] It did not matter whether or not it was a true or a fictional story, whether or not the movie characters were real people or just actors, whether the Hughes brothers or anyone else had lived the life they described. The film was executed in a way that made it real: "Everybody, the writers, the set designers, tapped into something true."[12] Jay-Z utilizes the realness of the movie to make the point that it is impossible to "fake emotional truth."[13]

Jay-Z gives clarity to what he means by fake emotional truth when he mentions that some of the greatest MCs move away from their own emotional truth, such as when an artist who does conscious rap does an

---

9. Jay-Z, *Decoded* (New York: Spiegel and Grau, 2011), 251.

10. Ibid., 248.

11. *Menace II Society* is a 1993 film and drama, the directorial debut of twin brothers Allen and Albert Hughes. It is set in South Central Los Angeles and follows the life of Caine Lawson and his close friends. *Menace II Society* was critically acclaimed for its gritty portrayal of urban violence and complex human motivations.

12. Jay-Z, *Decoded*, 248.

13. Ibid.

"ignorant joint," or when a classic party-starter MC starts doing gangsta rap and people know that it is not real. Undoubtedly, Jay-Z is referring to the enormously successful hip-hop rapper MC Hammer, who decided to harden his image, drop the MC from his name, and rap as a "gangsta." Overwhelmingly, the audience decided the move was an existentially inauthentic performance (fake emotional truth) and did not buy this form of his music. In this same vein, Jay-Z contends that many performers believe that they have to stray from their emotional truth to be successful. He tells a new and upcoming group that he has signed to his label that they should not try to make a hot radio single because, in this instance, that is not their emotional truth. He counsels them to make a great album from the first song to the last because faking emotional truth might work in the short term, but it is a "house of sand."[14] To be faithful to one's emotional truth is to be authentic to one's own art, to be real to one's experience and how that experience leads to the shaping of a rhyme, regardless of the lure of market forces.

In summary, according to rhetorical critic Jay-Z, the real is based upon how an MC shapes their experience into a rhyme, that is (1) the logic the lyrics follow, (2) the emotional truth that supports the lyrics, (3) the human motivations that the MC fills in, and (4) the commitment to getting even the smallest details right. I would like to explain how I understand each of these criteria Jay-Z suggests and utilize the concept of the real to discuss what excellence in black preaching is.

The Logic of the Lyrics

When Jay-Z says the logic of the lyrics are a part of keeping it real, then my interpretation is that he means two things. First is the way the rhyme or story is structured, that is, how the content of the plot or narrative is designed for maximum impact, effect, and feeling upon the listener. Let me illustrate my interpretation of structuring of the plot or narrative for maximum impact by discussing the lyrics to Jay-Z's song "Meet the Parents."[15]

---

14. Ibid., 249.
15. Ibid., 210.

CHAPTER FOUR

Jay-Z starts the song with a send-off, the burial and afterlife of a young hustler who was shot and killed. After he describes the rain-gray skies at the cemetery, and the forlorn cries of, "Such a good kid," he gives the audience the sense that the young man was honorable and well respected by his peers. He then shifts the narrative to talk about the single mother of the deceased hustler, Isis, who is not strong enough to raise a boy by herself, as many women are not, Jay-Z suggests and later amends, given the reality of the streets. The father's name was Shorty, who never knew the boy or tried to raise him.[16] After the death of her son, and seeing his body at the city morgue, Isis turned to drugs. Her addiction grew and grew until she lived in the land of drug-based fantasy. Jay-Z fully develops the character of Isis by suggesting that she, like so many young ladies in the ghetto, fell for the aggressive, violent, and exciting Shorty at sixteen. But, what is appealing at sixteen is not necessarily attractive when the thug becomes a grown man.

Jay-Z identifies the absent father (Shorty) as Mike. Mike has a son who is now fifteen, as Jay-Z reminds us again, whom he had disowned from birth. Fifteen years later, Mike is still on the streets, and he approaches this young thug. Both end up drawing .38-caliber guns. The younger is faster and has the drop on Mike, but the young son hesitates because the face looks familiar. Jay-Z adds, in his commentary about the lyrics, "You get the sense that he's studied every face he's seen looking for the face of his father. And now here it is. It freezes him."[17] He hesitates, but the father does not and kills his son. The song concludes with a repetition of the lyrics: "Six shots into his kin, out of the gun / Niggaz be a father, you're killin your son" and concludes with the title of the song.[18]

Jay-Z structures the plot of the rhyme for maximum effect and feeling by starting with the send-off and funeral, and then shows the audience how we got there. The afterlife becomes the prologue to turn the story on its head to emphasize that a father kills his children when he walks out on

---

16. "Shorty" is common lingo for "every" young brother, in the sense that the neighborhood is full of so many just like Shorty.

17. Jay-Z, *Decoded*, 211.

18. Ibid.

them. Notice the careful attention to the character development of, first, Isis. The death of her son led to her addiction and her love of thugs at sixteen flowers into the death of her son fifteen years later, the deepest pain of her life. Second, Shorty/Mike is the absentee father who never grows up, and is still running the streets fifteen years after the birth of his son. And third is the young son, on the streets, hard, perpetuating intergenerational schism by not feeling that he has to pay respect to the older generation, yet human enough to still be looking for his father's face. Jay-Z brings the entire narrative to resolution in the meeting of the father and son face to face and gun to gun. The father kills his own son. He closes with the admonition to be fathers because fathers who abandon their children are killing their sons. When he closes with the song's title, "Meet the Parents," he means that it is impossible to understand the hip-hop generation without understanding their parents. Jay-Z suggests that if one thinks the hip-hop generation is "messed up," meet their parents.

The field of homiletics would do well to study this kind of poetic genius to make better preachers. The narrative structure and character development, not to mention the descriptive imagery and wordplay, are worthy of imitation for anyone who wants to be effective at preaching. Also, a generation has grown up listening to hip-hop poetics, and based upon the inexorable march of time, these poetics have affected preaching, and certainly will continue to do so, as these young preachers approach their zenith in the pulpit. I issue this challenge and ask this question of the older generations of preachers: How can we support, learn from, develop, and mentor this generation, if we do not, at least, understand one of their major forms of proclamation? There are many things (i.e., narrative structure, character development, descriptive imagery, and wordplay) that older preachers can learn from this generation. The first part of realness of the logic of the lyrics is the content of the plot or narrative is designed for maximum impact, effect, and feeling upon the listener. Preachers would do well and gain more interest from their audience by giving more consideration to the structuring of their sermons for maximum impact, effect, and feeling upon the listener.

To get at the second aspect of realness, according to my interpretation of Jay-Z's logic of the lyrics, is to honestly address the profane side of life. Homiletics also could learn a great deal from hip-hop poetics on how to address the profane side of life. To get at this, the question must be asked: Do the lyrics of the hip-hop poet follow the logic of real life? Is it plausible that what the poet describes could happen in real life? Some argue that they could imagine a father meeting and killing his son face to face and gun to gun in Jay-Z's neighborhood, that is, the ghetto or urban America. The implication here, perpetrated by white supremacist notions of reality, is that this kind of violence only happens in the "hood," and not in the suburbs, small towns, and rural areas of America.[19]

This understanding of the ghetto is a form of denial based upon constructed mythology anchored in white privilege. Kane illustrates this point when he says: "Those 'keepin it real' have been historically and materially severed from the simulated suburban society that has become our national self-image. This separation is then perpetuated in the media that portrays as random the apparently senseless acts of violence that wear only a black mask."[20]

Patrick Sharkey, in his book *Stuck in Place: Urban Neighborhoods and the End of Progress toward Racial Equality*, looks beyond individual factors alone such as home, family structure, or culture affecting character, and argues that the inequality of the ghetto is the result of intentional social policy organized in space by the political, social, cultural, and economic institutions of American society. He argues that the social problems prevalent in America's ghettoes, among them the gun violence of Jay-Z's "Meet the Parents," "are the product of shortsighted policies, intentional efforts to isolate or exclude minority communities within cities, and ma-

---

19. I use the term *white supremacist* following Thomas Kane: "By *white supremacist*, I don't mean to suggest that the entire nation is wearing Klan gear or painting graffiti swastikas; instead, I intend the term to connote a *de facto* white supremacy, where the privilege of whiteness is assumed and perpetuated across generations so that taking the historically long view, the majority of property, wealth, and material goods are owned and operated for white profit. See Kane, "Bringing the Real: Lacan and Tupac," 661.

20. Ibid., 646.

jor economic and demographic shifts."[21] I would argue that while there are definitely aspects of personal responsibility and choice in the levels of violence, the political, social, cultural, and economic institutions of American society are not as innocent as many white-thinking institutions would lead us to believe.

The hip-hop poet knows that violence is not simply a matter of a lack of character of ghetto inhabitants, but visible and structural inequality that has deep roots in American racism. The hip-hop poet knows violence happens in every community and knows no boundary of race, ethnicity, or socioeconomics class. For example, parents are in the midst of divorce proceedings and the father comes to the door with a gun and kills the mother and three children, and then turns the gun on himself—"Six shots into his kin, out of the gun." A classmate brings an assault rifle to class and kills fourteen students and three teachers—"Six shots into his kin, out of the gun." And in response, it is often stated innocently in the media, "We never thought it would happen in our neighborhood, small town, or rural area." In truth, those in suburban, rural, and small-town areas end up discussing the same issues as Jay-Z in "Meet the Parents"—hopeless youth and adults feeling abandoned, isolated, alone, and violent, sometimes with mental-health issues and access to guns and ammunition. We are the parents and the violence is real in every neighborhood.

The violence is real, present in every neighborhood, except that in many sermons we do not like to talk of such things. If we are not careful, our religion will become neat, proper, respectful, sanctimonious, ceremonial, reserved, dignified, nonpolitical, holy, prosperous, and prosperity based, and giving evidence of our God-ordained social status and success. When those of the hip-hop community use holy profanity, they are validating their own experience, making space for black presence, and announcing that sometimes life is raw, dirty, contradictory, mistake-filled, ironic, vulgar, loud, tragic, complicated, conflicted, uncertain, painful, and desperate. They believe their reality is fundamentally human, and as a result, they are human. Therefore, they use profane God language to

---

21. Patrick Sharkey, *Stuck in Place: Urban Neighborhoods and the End of Progress toward Racial Equality* (Chicago: University of Chicago Press, 2013).

describe their profane human experience because they believe that their profane human lives are sacred.

Many churches and preachers, including some black churches and black preachers, do not like to discuss violence, "urban," "ghetto," or "big-city problems." We do not like to discuss what Phyllis Tribble calls the "texts of terror," such as the violence against four women in ancient Israel, Hagar (Gen 16:1-16), Tamar (2 Sam 13:1-19), an unnamed concubine (Judg 19:1-30), and the daughter of Jephthah (Judg 11:1-40).[22] We do not like to talk about the violence of human cruelty in the Bible, the apparent silence of God, and other texts that sanction rape, conquest, genocide, slavery, assassination, beheading, and the like.

Admittedly, these are difficult texts to preach, but in the meantime, while we ignore the profane side of life, rapes, molestations, murders, corporate greed, sexual violence, wealth inequality, hunger, poverty, unemployment, lack of educational opportunity, white-collar crime, drive-by shootings, relationship violence, addictions, police violence, and the social and spiritual death that is all around us go fundamentally unaddressed. Far too many sermons will not deal with it. Far too many sermons are based in the constructed mythology of the media-based simulated American life. Far too much of the preaching of our time is safe, the standard fare of what many of us have come to expect to hear when we go to church: God as our life coach to help us improve our relationships, finances, and health. Homiletics would do well to learn from hip-hop poetics to address the real—the inexorable profane side of life. And sometimes life is so profane that the most appropriate way to share our feelings and understandings is holy profanity.

My argument is, because the church will not address the real, many people turn away from the church to what they deem as "real" in movies, television, entertainment, sports, money, sex, and the like. If they cannot find the real, at least they can have a real escape. In research and preparation for the writing of this chapter, I watched a DVD of a Jay-Z concert. It was amazing the mix of people who were there. It was amazing how

---

22. Phyllis Tribble, *Texts of Terror: Literary-Feminist Readings of Biblical Narratives* (Minneapolis: Fortress Press, 1984).

many there were of the "non-ghetto crowd." There were some kids from the suburbs, small towns, and rural areas with their gold chains on and hats turned to the side, baggy pants and all. There were some executives and members of the corporate crowd there with "their hands raised in the air, acting like they just don't care." There were some hustlers there. There were some single mothers there. The ghetto crowd was there. And you know what amazed me—they were all mouthing the lyrics right along with Jay-Z. It was amazing. They knew the lyrics to all the songs. I must admit that I was jealous—if we could get them to mouth scripture the way that they were reciting those lyrics, the church could be relevant again. Maybe Jay-Z is mouthing what we preachers need to mouth—the real. Maybe Jay-Z is offering an existentially authentic performance.

Oh yes! I forgot to mention who else was there at the concert—Isis was there; Shorty/Mike was there; and the young thug son was there—they all left the church, looking for the real. Why can't they find the real in church? People are looking for an existentially authentic performance where the logic in the lyrics also reflects the profane side of life because all hearers, to one extent or another, experience the profane side of life, whether by racism, illness, death, broken relationships, war, violence, death, or some other way. The profane side of life is part of human life and why we find the profane so often in the Bible. If the profane is the Bible, and the profane is in life, then why not is the profane in our sermons?

THE EMOTIONAL TRUTH THAT SUPPORTS THE LYRICS

After the logic of the lyrics, the second criterion of realness of an existentially authentic performance is the emotional truth that supports the lyrics. As I understand it, emotional truth as defined by Jay-Z is similar to a concept that I teach in my preaching classes that, following Nicholas Cooper-Lewter and Henry H. Mitchell in their book *Soul Theology*, I label *core belief*. They define core belief as

> the bedrock attitudes that govern all deliberate behavior and relationships and also all spontaneous responses to crises . . . core beliefs are our working opinions about whether God can be trusted. . . . They have

been acquired through life experiences, worship, and cultural exposure, and they can be altered likewise. Core beliefs are not mere propositions to which assent is given. They are the ways one trusts or fails to trust. They are embraced intuitively and emotionally, without the ability to express them rationally. Core beliefs are perhaps most authentically expressed when uttered spontaneously in crisis situations.[23]

Cooper-Lewter and Mitchell are writing from a spiritual perspective, explaining the theology and core beliefs of the African American community, but I believe everyone has a core belief, whether or not they consider themselves religious. Core belief in this sense is the way in which one trusts or fails to trust. We all have life and cultural experiences that shape belief, what and whom we trust and do not trust. It is these beliefs that form the foundation for all our behavior and relationships. Every living and breathing human being has a core belief. Jay-Z would say the emotional truth (core belief) that supports the lyrics makes the lyrics real. I say that the expression of core belief (emotional truth) that undergirds the message makes the sermon real.

What I have noticed is that many preachers seem to not clearly know their core belief, or maybe are unable to express them in a sermon, that is, what they most deeply believe. One of my critiques of most seminary education is that we professors are much better at helping students explore doubt and skepticism, and not as good at spiritual formation and helping students to come to know what they deeply believe. We are better at intellectual doubt than we are the formation of heartfelt trust and core belief. Far too many students come out of seminary not sure and certain about what they believe. I know that I am painting many people with a broad brush, but my experience was that after my seminary education deconstructed my belief system, it took me seven years in the pastorate to put the pieces together to know what I believed. Many suggest that my experience was a natural process that every student must go through of integrating what we learn in seminary with the practical realities of

---

23. Nicholas C. Cooper-Lewter and Henry H. Mitchell, *Soul Theology: The Heart of American Black Culture* (San Francisco: Harper & Row Publishers, 1986), 3.

people's lives that we relate to in congregational life.[24] Maybe integration does takes time, but in the meantime, I tell my students this: *preach what you deeply believe because people have enough of their own doubts and do not need yours.* I define knowing what you believe as core belief.

I developed an exercise that I take the students through that helps them articulate core belief. I recount to them an experience when I served as pastor of a local congregation, a situation of church conflict that was extremely difficult and painful for many, and as a result, a very difficult preaching environment. I told them that rather than address the situation directly, I decided to preach the character of God. I told them in their times of the most difficult agony, anger, struggle, disappointment, and heartache to set all that aside and preach what they believe most deeply about the character of God. With that information as preface, I then ask them, *What do you believe most deeply about the character of God?*

Typically, I move to the chalkboard/white board and record their responses. Often, I write "God is love," "God is always present," and various other qualities of the character of God, such as mercy, kindness, faithfulness, truth, and grace. Because the exercise is usually emotionally intense, in that people go deeply interior to respond, we all take a deep breath and survey the responses on the board.

After a few minutes, I ask them a second question: *How did you come to know what you believe most deeply about the character of God?* Undoubtedly, most students will recount some experience. It was through an experience, often painful, that they came to know what they know about the character of God. Sometimes tears flow in class because these experiences are again deeply emotional. For example, I remember a student who shared with tears in his eyes an account of being abandoned in a divorce and the attending feelings of guilt and shame. He recounted meditating on John 14:18 (NIV), where Jesus tells the disciples, "I will not leave you

---

24. Many mainline Protestant seminaries in North America are heavily influenced by the Paris/Berlin paradigm that views seminary education as primarily a "form of developing literate, critical, scholarly expertise." Seminary is an experience that is away from the church, cloistered in a way quite appropriate for scholarly, largely text-based learning to the exclusion of other models such as apprenticeship, small group, and experiential learning. See Matthew Myer Boulton's "The City of God & City of Cain," *Sojourner's*, September–October 2013, https://sojo.net/magazine/september-october-2013/city-god-city-cain.

as orphans; I will come to you." Though he knew that Jesus was talking to the disciples about his leaving and that was not a divorce, still their feelings of abandonment applied to his situation, and he experienced the comfort and the faithfulness of God in the words of Jesus and the removal of the feelings of guilt and shame. He had said in response to the earlier question about the character of God that God was faithful.

Core belief (emotional truth) is often generated by scripture, that is, Bible reading, meditation, prayer, and exegesis applied to lived human experience with the resulting joy, victory, sorrow, and pain. I tell the preaching students over and over again: *Preach what you deeply believe.* Preach the scripture that you have deeply lived human experience with. What I know is that when we preach what we deeply believe, our preaching has an existential authenticity to it—it is real.

I do not mean that we should only preach the texts that we have deep experience with or that we bring scripture down to the level of human experience. I do mean that we must come to a real place with every text that we preach. The text has realness, an existential authenticity, or core beliefs based upon the writers and writers' community lived experience with God. It is our task to exegete realness and core belief in the text, the lived human experience of the writers and the writers' community with God, and at the same time, our human experience with God and our core belief to help the listener understand and articulate their own experience with God and core belief. It means that we do not always follow the latest and greatest preaching trend or fad, which is to fake emotional truth. Or, that we slavishly imitate the preaching and core belief of someone else, though all of us are influenced by mentors and high-quality preachers. We must be careful that we explore our own humanity, the depths of our own experience and core belief.

It might be that because we have not exegeted the experience of the writers of scripture and the writer's community with God, their core belief, or exegeted our own experience with God, or our community's experience with God and core belief, that our preaching has lost its vitality and fire. We offer fake emotional truth as our preaching takes intellectual flight well above the heads, experiences, and understanding of the people, as the people wonder what exactly is the point, or offer emotionally charged clichés and superficial phrases that function as cotton candy in the mouths of the listeners that tastes good on Sunday, but does not connect their lives to the real experience of the biblical text during the week. We can offer more style than substance; more heat than light; more pleasure than truth. Tired of preaching that is not real, that lacks authenticity and honesty about human experience, people look to the real in music, movies, entertainment, sports, sex, work, Oprah's Sunday morning programming, and a host of other possibilities. People are looking for something to believe in at their core, or someone who believes something at their core and can communicate it to help listeners discover their core belief. If preaching does not keep it real, and loses emotional truth/core belief, then it loses the existentially authentic performance, and runs the risk, in Jay-Z's words, of going the way of disco and the blues.

THE HUMAN MOTIVATION THE MC FILLS IN

The third criterion that Jay-Z mentions for the real is the human motivation that the MC fills in. It is important to notice the qualifier before the word *motivation*—*human*. It is the *human* motivation that the MC fills in. The word *human* suggests something broad, large, and common to humanity and the general human experience. When the MC shapes a rhyme and develops a character in the rhyme, the MC supplies motivations to the characters, and if the motivations are large and broad enough, then they become human and understandable to a broad base of listeners.

In our aforementioned discussion of "Meet the Parents," for example, Jay-Z supplies motivation to the young son as to why, though he has the drop on his father, he does not shoot: the face looks familiar and the boy has studied every face looking for his father's face. Looking for the face of one's father is human, especially for those who have been abandoned, and therefore large enough and broad enough to be understandable to a general base of listeners.

Jay-Z defined the purpose of his music, from his first to his latest album, as the desire to articulate "the interior space of a young kid's head, his psychology."[25] He means that a kid does not wake up one day and say, "I think I will sell drugs today." It is hard for many to see the inner motivation of a young kid selling drugs (hustling), but there is a context, a specific motivation, an inner psychology, and some purposeful action, even if we do not agree with the moral choice of selling drugs and the like. He suggests that to negatively identify, or demonize and stereotype a kid who sells drugs, or a kid who has a gun, and not clarify why the kid sells drugs or has the gun in the first place is to tell a type of a lie. It is not the full story. In his analysis of the psychology of a hustler, he says, "Hustling is the ultimate metaphor for the basic human struggle; the struggle to survive and resist, the struggle to win and make sense of it all."[26] Hustling is human and if the MC is skilled enough, the MC's struggle to survive and resist becomes the struggle of every person. This is why, Jay-Z would argue, hip-hop has reached a worldwide audience: "This is why the hustler's story—through hip-hop—has connected with a global audience. The deeper we get into those sidewalk cracks and into the mind of the young hustler trying to find his fortune there, the closer we get to the ultimate human story, the story of struggle, which is what defines us all."[27]

Realness has to do with motivations and the ability of the MC to see and describe motivations that are fundamentally human, and therefore common to us all.

Now, let me try to drop all of this into homiletical terms. I tell my students that when we push our human experience deep enough it goes universal. When I use the term *push*, I mean when we examine, observe, interpret, and look critically at our own human experience; we might find themes, concerns, and joys that are common to the human family. If we are insightful and descriptive enough, often it goes deep enough to become universal, that is, applicable to a broad range of the human family. For example, my particularity is that I am an African American male and because of that African American maleness, I have a particular set of lived human experiences. When I get into my own inner psychology, see and

---

25. Jay-Z, *Decoded*, 17.

26. Ibid., 18.

27. Ibid., 19.

understand my deepest experiences and motivations, those experiences sometimes are large enough to reach a broad base of listeners. Let me give you an example of what I mean.

In the quietness, serenity, and intimacy of my study as a pastor, I was told the essence of this story that I am going to relate by one of my then congregants. I have changed and embellished several critical factors to protect any possibility of anyone identifying who I am talking about, or anyone who has talked to me being able to identify themselves. The story has been changed to protect the innocent.

A son determines to tell his father that he is a same-sex, gender-loving person. He has rehearsed it a thousand times, what he would say, and how he would say it. The time for the lunch with his father comes. As he sits at the table and finishes his main course, he notices that the time is slipping away, and he is having a hard time getting it out. Dessert is finished, and as he reaches to pay the bill, he knows that it is now or never—he blurts out, "Dad, I have a partner." The silence is absolute. The son waits and notices that he is sweating now, his pulse is up, and his breathing is rapid. The father finally speaks, "No fag is a son of mine." With anger and hostility, he says at the top of his lungs, "You are no son of mine." The father slams his napkin on the table and storms off. The son is left sitting there, broken and in tears.

Now, it is possible to talk about this story-example from many perspectives. We could, for example, discuss the theological issue of whether or not a same-gender relationship is a sin according to the Bible. I choose to talk about it much different than that. I choose to talk about it from the perspective of human experience. I look at it from the viewpoint of the son's inner motivation to tell someone important to him, his father in this case, his true identity and have it accepted. It is a common human yearning that we try to tell someone important to us who we really are and hope that they can hear it. Maybe it is a sister, brother, friend, wife, husband, employer, childhood friend, fellow church member, or family member. Have you ever tried to tell someone who you really were, or some aspect of yourself that was really important to you, and they could not hear it? Have you ever tried to reveal your true feelings to someone and were summarily rejected, or on the other hand, had the awesome experience of someone hearing you, and both you and your feelings were unconditionally accepted? David Augsburger said that being listened to is so close to being loved that we can hardly tell the difference.[28] One way or the other, if not both, most of us have had these human experiences. If the son would push his experience of rejection deep enough, he would find that there are many of us who have been rejected in some similar manner. Have you ever tried to tell someone who you really were?

Can we look at our own deepest motivations and see them in others? Can we read the biblical text and see deep human motivation? Can we look beneath the surface of the macho bravado in "Meet the Parents" and see that a young hustler might still be looking for his father? In a sermon entitled "Renew Your Yes," I ascribe human motivation to Eli, the priest who was under judgment from God, and ultimately replaced by Samuel, based upon the fact that he could not discipline his two sons, Hophni and Phineas. While it is easy to judge Eli for being a bad parent, I thought about the fact that those of us who are seasoned in ministry, in the middle to the closing years of our ministry, come to know the same judgment of God on our ministry that Eli experienced, and I wrote these words:

> Eli is a good priest, but not a good parent. He will not discipline his sons. All of us have short-comings; all of us make mistakes; all of us have places where were we struggle to meet the standard. . . . Some of us have saved other people's children, but could not save our own. . . . We are good priests. . . . We minister the Word, share the sacraments, commit ashen bodies back unto the Lord, bless babies, and consummate weddings. We walk hospital floors, sometime in the wee hours of the morning, pray when the diagnosis is cancer, pass handkerchiefs and Kleenex when the tears are flowing fast and furious, bring hope to the hopeless, and are a friend to the friendless. We rail against injustices against the poor, declare righteousness where there is oppression, decry sin and disobedience to God, and we sit in courtrooms with members who have made mistakes. Despite all of this, we know that there are places where our ministry has not measured up. We know we have faults, flaws, mis-

---

28. David Augsburger, "Quotable Quote," http://www.goodreads.com/quotes/288161-being-heard-is-so-close-to-being-loved-that-for.

takes, and shortcomings. . . . There is more that we could have accomplished. This is the anguish of those of us who are seasoned. This is the anguish of Eli.[29]

Many midcareer ministers know what it means to experience judgment from God on our ministries. Maybe it is not as severe judgment as Eli, but many of us know the anguish of Eli.

When it is real, the motivations are right and authentic. The poet and the preacher, by making the human motivations broad and large enough, help us to see the same motivations in the text and within ourselves. The ability of the preacher to supply common human motivations is critical if the sermon is to be real.

GETTING EVEN THE SMALLEST DETAIL RIGHT

Returning to Jay-Z's earlier comments in this chapter about the movie *Menace II Society*, you will remember that he mentions that initially he had no idea whether the Hughes Brothers, who co-directed the film, actually lived the life portrayed in the film, or if anyone else did either, but the opening scene convinced him that it was real. It was the right details that convinced him: "the way the smoke filled that red-lit room," or "Marvin Gaye soul spinning on the turntable." He said the look the son had on his face when the father's guns started blazing—no one could fake that emotional truth. Though the movie was a fictional story, with actors, not real people, he said the execution of the film made it real. The writers, actors, and set designers "tapped into something true." It can be fiction, fantasy, or complete and absolute truth; the poet has to ground the rhyme in details that made them real to the audience. Homiletics could learn this from hip-hop poetics: the preacher must be committed to get even the smallest details right because right details make the story real.

Henry H. Mitchell sums up the entire process and effect of the right detail by labeling it *identification*. The best preachers select right details and create identification:

---

29. Frank A. Thomas, *The Choice: Living Your Passion Inside Out* (Indianapolis, IN: Hope for Life Press, 2013), 76–77.

CHAPTER FOUR

> The preacher needs *carefully* to select vivid details. Oft times it is the details which determine how deeply involved the hearer will be. . . . The associations called forth may be emotionally cathartic and healing of pain; they may be feelings of righteous indignation; or they may be joyous, irrepressible waves of praise and celebration. Whatever the character of the response deep emotions are moved to expression by identification with familiar specifics of place, problem, or other detail.[30]

The detail that the preacher selects to place in the sermon directly affects the amount of identification the preacher creates. Good storytellers, preachers, poets, and others are committed to getting even the smallest details right. Too few details and the audience does not have enough to identify with and get on board with the story. I have heard stories and sermons without enough details to trigger our senses, and when our senses are not triggered, there is no identification, and when there is no identification, no emotion is released, and when no emotion is released, no interest is gained. I have heard stories and sermons with too little sense appeal and virtually no interest from the audience.

On the other hand, I have heard sermons with too many details and the story bogs down into minutiae and the audience is confused as to what is important and why the story is being told. I have seen preachers get lost and wander in their own stories, and even forget their basic point, based upon too much detail. The balance between too few and too many details can be called the "right detail," and it is impossible to have the right detail without a commitment to getting even the smallest details right.

When we do not give attention to getting the smallest details right, it is a form of either undisciplined inattention or tragic laziness, and it dramatically diminishes the audiences' experience. Recently, I went to see a movie that was set in the 1960s. The producers were careful to insure that every detail of the movie was true to the 1960s. Imagine a scene in the movie from the 1960s and the music in the background is from the 1990s. The audience will perceive the incongruence and automatically know the scene is either comedic or not real. The details must be exact and true to the 1960s and the only way they are exact and true is if attention is given

---

30. Henry H. Mitchell, *Celebration and Experience in Preaching* (Nashville: Abingdon Press, 1990), 34.

to rigorous research, examination, and close observation of the context. So must it be with those who shape rhymes, sermons, and poems. When the smallest details are right, the rhyme becomes real. As a matter of fact, it can become so real that it does not matter, as we said earlier, if it is fiction or fact, if it actually happened or was made up, whether the preacher lived it or is telling someone else's story. The story, rhyme, or sermon is executed in such a way that the preacher and the audience tap into something true. It is the commitment to get even the smallest details right that makes the story real.

Let me illustrate the commitment to getting the right details and the smallest detail right by returning to Gardner C. Taylor's classic sermon that we discussed in the last chapter, "His Own Clothes." In another version of the sermon, Taylor describes the scene where Pilate turns Jesus over to his military detachment, the Praetorian Guard, for crucifixion:

> So one of the fellas ran out and got a cane, a reed, and stuck it in his hands. And they stripped him of his own clothes and one of them went and got an old cloak, a faded, purple cloak, which was a part of the uniform of the Roman soldier on dress parade. But this was an old, tattered, faded purple cloak . . . having taken off his own clothes, they flung the old cloak around his shoulders and one fella more daring than the others went outside and along the walls of the barracks, found a thorn bush, cut it with his sword, platted it into a crown, and came back and jammed it on the head of the Savior until rivulets of blood began running down his brow. And then in mock worship, they bowed down before him and said, "We hail you, king." And then, gales of laughter, wicked, scornful, laughter rang and reverberated through the barracks, beat against the wall, and echoed back.[31]

The right detail and the commitment to the smallest detail could be evidenced in many examples from this sermon excerpt, but I will only mention a few.

First, of all the details that could be relayed, Taylor chooses the right detail by letting the listener know that the purple cloak was part of the

---

31. Gardner C. Taylor, "In His Own Clothes," in *Preaching with Sacred Fire: An Anthology of African American Preaching, 1750 to the Present*, ed. Martha Simmons and Frank A. Thomas (New York: W. W. Norton & Company, 2010), 833.

uniform of the Roman soldier on dress parade. This was the fruit of his exegesis to ensure that he understood the biblical scene, as far as it was possible, to the smallest details. The purple cloak was normal raiment in the dress parade of the Roman soldier, which made the cloak regal, with vibrant purple color, and connects it with the disciplined exactness of military uniforms marching in victorious procession. Taylor contrasts this with the old, faded purple cloak that was put on Jesus. He mentions the adjectives *old, tattered,* and *faded* to paint the picture of their ridicule. These descriptors that appeal to the senses of the listeners create identification and stir emotion and interest in the hearer.

Second, again he paints the picture with the right details that stir the senses, releases emotion, and gains interest. Notice the descriptors, *thorn bush, cut* it with a sword, *jammed* it on the head, and *rivulets* of blood running down. Again, there are millions of details that Taylor could relay about the scene, but he selects the right details to put the listener in the scene and makes it such that one can actually see rivulets of blood running down his brow.

Finally, after mocking him in worship and hailing him as king, the sarcastic drama concludes with *gales of laughter, wicked, scornful, laughter rang and reverberated through the barracks, beat against the wall, and echoed back.* Notice that their wicked, scornful laughter *rang, reverberated, and beat against the wall, and echoed.* Because it is the right detail, I actually hear the scornful laughter reverberating. Taylor has placed me directly in the scene. The scene is not back there in biblical times; it is happening right in front of me. I feel their bitterness, see the blood run down his brow, and hear the wicked laughter beat against the walls and echo. And all of this is done not counting volume, tone, pace, inflection, facial expression, and so on, much of which is left out in our reading of the text rather than hearing or seeing the sermon preached. This is the importance of commitment to getting even the smallest details right and the right detail: it makes the sermon real even if one reads it without the dynamics of live delivery. Would that preachers could spend this kind of time and energy, getting even the smallest details right, putting listeners in the scene, our preaching would come alive being fresh, relevant, and for the audience—an existentially authentic performance.

Communicative expression encompasses the study of black preaching through the examination of black sacred rhetoric, inclusive of music, poetry, hip-hop, public discourse, new media, and other cultural forms. Valerie Bridgeman's identification of the potential of the poetic form in contemporary preaching suggests that homiletics can learn and shape criteria for effective preaching from hip-hop poetics. While I agree with Bridgeman's comment that the "next, natural step" in preaching is the "poetic sermonic form," it does not mean that I expect every sermon to be in the poetic sermon form.[32] What I do expect is that excellence in preaching will be much more heavily influenced by poetic form, such as in Jay-Z's terms, the validity of the existentially authentic performance to include, the logic the lyrics follow, the emotional truth that supports the lyrics, the human motivations that the MC fills in, and the commitment to getting even the smallest details. There is a tremendous amount that homiletics can learn from the poetic generation and contemporary poetry in hip-hop music. Let the dialogue continue.

---

32. O. Wesley Allen, Jr., ed. *The Renewed Homiletic*, "Celebration Renewed," 63.

Chapter Five
THE TRUTH IS ALWAYS RELEVANT:

Race and Economics in Contemporary African American Preaching

It is important that we conclude by considering possible future trends in black preaching. In the last chapter, "'Keepin' It Real:' The Validity of the Existentially Authentic Performance," we discussed the poetic sermonic form as the next, natural step in African American homiletics. The discussion of the poetic sermonic form was a glimpse of what *form* African American preaching might take. In this chapter, I would like to discuss future trends in black preaching, specifically speaking to the question of the relevancy of the *content* of black preaching to the African American Millennial generation. Many of this present generation of young African American people, who by and large still remain in the church, have defined the most relevant subjects as police violence, brutality, and accountability, or as Khalil Gibran Muhammad said, "The right to not die prematurely."[1] The issue of police violence in the black community is intricately connected to issues of race and economics, and many Millennials look for the church to address and confront the issues directly.

This chapter will explore how the black church can engage, assist, and reach Millennials, who seek the reemergence of mass social justice

---

1. Khalil Gibran Muhammad, "The Revolution Will Be Live-Tweeted: Why #BlackLives Matter Is the New Model for Civil Rights," *The Guardian*, December 1, 2014, accessed February 5, 2015; available at www.theguardian.com/commentisfree/2014/dec/01/black-lives-matter-civil-rights-movement-ferguson.

movements. If the African American church does not address race and economics, or is not thoughtful and skilled in addressing these issues, Millennials will consider the church not relevant to their lives, needs, and struggles. Will the relevance of twenty-first-century sermons and churches be obvious and empowering to the burgeoning mass social justice movements of today? Will the church and its preaching be relevant to Millennials? For those earnestly longing to be relevant, I want to explore Jay-Z's comment that "the truth is always relevant."

The Truth Is Always Relevant

The aforementioned hip-hop and business mogul Jay-Z, in his critically acclaimed and surprisingly exegetical tour de force, *Decoded*, makes this penetrating statement: "For hip hop to grow to its potential and stay relevant for another generation we have to keep pushing deeper and deeper into the biggest subjects and doing it with real honesty. The truth is always relevant."[2]

The context of Jay-Z's comments is that he believes that musical genres can die because they lose their "signature and vitality," and other musical forms "steal their fire." From Jay-Z's perspective, ultimately these genres will experience demise and go the way of disco and the blues. Some would debate the demise of the blues, but his point is if hip-hop is to stay relevant to another generation, it must push deeper and deeper into the biggest subjects with real honesty. Jay-Z's insightful maxim is that facing the biggest subjects with real depth and honesty brings truth, and truth is always relevant.

As a teacher of preaching, I have applied Jay-Z's statement to churches, seminaries, and denominations who are trying to figure out how to stay relevant amidst the painful decline of mainline churches and religious institutions in a postmodern culture that is increasingly secular, diverse, and non-traditional. For many Millennials and Gen-Xers, the church is not a priority, and as a result, white American Millennials are nonaffiliating in alarmingly large numbers. My paraphrase of Jay-Z is to suggest that churches, seminaries, and denominations must push deeper and deeper

---

2. Jay-Z, *Decoded* (New York: Spiegel and Grau, 2011), 277.

into the biggest subjects, with real honesty. If not, then religious institutions will be pushed further to the fringe of culture and society, and eventually to the place of anachronism and irrelevancy.

If this occurs, that is, religious institutions are pushed to the fringe, then some of the lack of relevancy will be expressed in and as a result of the preaching. If preaching does not engage the biggest subjects with real depth and honesty, then preaching itself will go the way of disco and the blues. Black preaching will go the way of the comedic caricatures from television shows and movies characterizing black preaching, such as in the classic film *The Blues Brothers*. Preaching and preachers will be respected for their comedic entertainment value as emotional relief, or ceremonial chaplains for invocations, weddings, funerals, dire emergencies, and in time of national crisis such as war, mass shootings, and terrorism. But they will not be consulted and valued for the most important ongoing civic, social, political, economic, and spiritual issues of the lives of young people. If the church does not move from exclusion to inclusion and diversity, from insistence on gradualism and patience to sensing, in Martin Luther King Jr.'s words, "the fierce urgency of now," then the church will not be pertinent in the lives of young people.[3] If the church does not move from charismatic leadership to collaboration, from a focus on appeasing conservative ideology in the church and the nation to listening and responding positively to the pain, hurt, anger, and activism of the new movement, then the church will be not valued or valuable. The church will be a relic and holdover from an old worldview that refuses to face new twenty-first-century flattened hierarchies and consensus-building social media reality.

After witnessing the killing of so many unarmed young black men and women by police, and in several cases non-police, young people are saying clearly and loudly, "Enough is enough." They have formed their own dispersed movement, most visibly known as Black Lives Matter, but with many other coalitions and organizations as well, such as Dream Defenders, Coalition Against Police Violence, Black Youth Project 100, Tribe X, and Lost Voices. And not just within the borders of the United States.

---

3. Martin Luther King, Jr. "I Have a Dream" speech, August 28, 1963, http://www.americanrhetoric.com/speeches/mlkihaveadream.htm

Black Lives Matter has become a global movement stretching to Palestine, Canada, and Ghana, as Janaya Khan says: "Black Lives Matter has become a transformative outlet for all black people from different historical, cultural, socioeconomic and political identities. It is a source of solidarity for the survivors of colonization, exploitation, capitalism and police brutality."[4]

Are religious institutions—inclusive of churches, denominations, and seminaries—relevant to these organizations? How relevant is our preaching in black churches to this movement? And, if a preacher wants to be relevant to this movement, how and what would the preacher preach? Let's begin by contrasting the civil rights movement of the 1950s and 1960s with our present new movement of primarily African American young people.

The Civil Rights Movement and the New Movement

There are many references comparing the new movement to the civil rights movement of the 1950s and 1960s. Through dynamic and relevant preaching that empowered activism, the civil rights movement flourished, broke the back of segregation, and brought significant change to American society. It is virtually indisputable that preaching was central and vital to the civil rights movement. While the preaching and addresses of Martin Luther King Jr. was almost exclusively foregrounded, there were many other preachers who activated people to make change, including Prathia Hall, Wyatt Tee Walker, Joseph Lowry, Andrew Young, Gardner C. Taylor, Walter E. Fauntroy, Jesse Jackson, C. T. Vivian, Ralph Abernathy, and many others. There were civil rights campaigns with other organizations doing additional and complementary work, but the media focused primarily on King.

It is also important to acknowledge that not all African American churches were involved in civil rights. Though the black church's participation in the civil rights movement is claimed today by the vast majority

---

4. Janaya Khan, "Black Lives Matter Has Become a Global Movement," *The Root*, August 7, 2015, accessed November 11, 2015; available from www.theroot.com/articles/culture/2015/08/black_lives_matter_has_become_a_global_movement.html.

of African American preachers and churches, many preachers were silent from their pulpits, and some were highly critical of King and the civil rights movement. The most vivid example of such opposition is J. H. Jackson, the president of the National Baptist Convention, USA, Inc. (NBC) from 1953 to 1982, the largest predominantly African American Christian denomination in the United States, and the world's second largest Baptist denomination. Jackson consistently, publicly, and vociferously advocated against the civil rights movement. Wallace Best suggests that "Jackson was a complex and paradoxical individual who exhibited an array of shifting political stances throughout his long career."[5] Jackson supported civil rights legislation with President Eisenhower in 1956, but in part, as Best documents, because of the rivalry with King, Jackson was a rigorous opponent of the mainstream civil rights movement. A small minority of preachers—black, white, Jewish, and otherwise—led the chorus for change that came to be known as the civil rights movement.

Within the struggles for civil rights, there were tensions and tussles between younger leaders and the older and more traditional leaders, King in particular. The Student Non-violent Coordinating Committee (SNCC) had tremendous conflicts with King and others about tactics, publicity, and what SNCC acknowledged as the hierarchical leadership of King and his associates. Besides conflicts with SNCC, one of the biggest struggles in the black community was one of philosophy and tactics: the nonviolence of King and the church and the nationalistic and black power tactics represented in Malcolm X, the Nation of Islam, and others. In 1966, Stokely Carmichael, also known as Kwame Ture, was the leader of SNCC, and launched the phrase "Black Power" in national consciousness, seeking to force King to take a position for black power. Nationalists and black power advocates did not agree with the tactics of moral suasion and appealing to the conscience of white America, since, in their opinion, that had been tried without result for centuries since the beginning of the Trans-Atlantic slave trade to America. They believed that black pride, self-determination, self-protection, and black economics would

---

5. Wallace Best,"The Right Achieved and the Wrong Way Conquered": J. H. Jackson, Martin Luther King, Jr., and the Conflict over Civil Rights," *Religion and American Culture: A Journal of Interpretation* 16, no. 2 (Summer 2006): 195–226.

yield African Americans the respect due to them as citizens of the United States of America. This present tension between younger and more nationalist and aggressive leadership of the new movement, and older, more traditional and patient approaches of the church is not by any means new. It has been debated since the advent of black struggles for freedom and will continue to be debated into the foreseeable future.

Acknowledging that these same tensions exist today, let's look at what might be the most significant subjects in the new movement that require the levels of depth and honesty with which Jay-Z speaks for the church to be relevant for Millennials and Gen-Xers. Let's search for the truth that is always relevant.

THE BIGGER SUBJECTS FOR MILLENNIALS AND GEN-XERS

With the acquittal of George Zimmerman for the shooting death of the African American teenager Trayvon Martin, the issue of violence against black youth was reignited and galvanized outrage and mass protests. The issue of violence against black people and black youth has always been a critical issue that has never been far below the surface of concern and activism in the black community. Protests in opposition to violence against blacks can be traced from and through the epoch of slavery and fugitive slave laws, the era of Jim Crow segregation and lynching, the period of "law and order" and war on drugs, to this present time of the new Jim Crow, the mass incarceration and killing of unarmed black people. Throughout American history, blacks have resisted state-sponsored and state-sanctioned terrorism, murder, brutality, and violence by slave patrols, night watches, sheriffs, and police, as well as vigilante para-police violence (i.e., riot mobs, lynch mobs, White Citizen Councils, the Klan).

These issues have been protested for redress in so many ways and instances that I mention only a few in the twentieth century. As we mentioned in the rhetorical analysis of Gardner C. Taylor's "His Own Clothes" (chapter 3), Billie Holiday sang "Strange Fruit," protesting the violence of and inhumanity of lynching. Gil Scott-Heron said, in "The Revolution Will Not Be Televised," that "there will be no pictures of pigs shooting down Brothers on the instant replay."[6] The Black Panthers listed in their Ten-Point Program, "We want an immediate end to police brutality and murder of black people."[7] NWA stirred major cultural polemics by controversial lyrics of protesting police brutality and racial profiling in late 1980s and 1990s. Constitution, state, and court-sanctioned overpolicing, and para-policing, of the black community has been an ongoing and continued issue of tension and struggle for generation upon generation in the black community.

But the acquittal of George Zimmerman was a tipping point and beyond what many young people could bear in the contemporary moment of the black freedom struggle. A movement emerged around the hashtag #BlackLivesMatter on social media. One year after the acquittal of Zimmerman, Michael Brown was shot and killed by a police officer in Ferguson, Missouri, who fired twelve times at an unarmed teenager. When a grand jury announced that Officer Darren Wilson would face no indictment, the movement against police violence grew in greater intensity and fervor. A further rash of deaths of unarmed young black people—Sandra Bland, Tamir Rice, Tony Robinson, Rekia Boyd, Walter Scott, and Eric Garner, to name a few—proved the nature of structural racism, violence, and brutality that had to be reformed. Diverse acts of defiance were launched. Bree Newsome climbed a flagpole to bring down a Confederate flag after the killing of nine people by a racist young man in Emmanuel African Methodist Episcopal Church, in Charleston, South Carolina. Undeniably, many young black people in America are in a state of protest and have formed their own twenty-first-century movement without consultation of traditional civil rights groups such as Rainbow Push, Social Action Network, NAACP, The Urban League, and others.

Rahiel Tesfamariam, social activist and former columnist for the *Washington Post*, wearing a representative T-shirt that said "This Ain't Yo Mama's Civil Rights Movement," was arrested in Ferguson, Missouri, in

---

6. Gil Scott-Heron, "The Revolution Will Not Be Televised," accessed December 1, 2015; available from www.metrolyrics.com/the-revolution-will-not-be-televised-lyrics-gil-scottheron.html.

7. Ten Point Program, http://www.pbs.org/hueypnewton/.

an act of civil disobedience for blocking the entrance to the St. Louis federal court. Tesfamariam summarizes the new movement:

> In the streets of Ferguson and Baltimore, the new movement for black lives was radicalized by legions of poor and working-class youth who forced the nation to grapple with black rage. They fearlessly confronted a militarized police force, tear gas, snipers and tanks designed for warfare.... These young people, including countless women and LGBTQ people who have organized many of the movement's most powerful acts of resistance, have changed the predominant image of black activism in America.[8]

As stated earlier, though the new movement is diverse, the public face of the movement tends to be Black Lives Matter. Representative of this new movement, in a September 2015 PBS-Marist poll, 59 percent of white Americans said that Black Lives Matter is a distraction and, in response to a separate question, 41 percent said it advocates violence (16 percent said they were unsure whether it does).[9] In my discussion with young activists, I do not believe white America's response to the new movement matters to them. They expect such, given the long history of structural racism, denial, innocence, and violence perpetrated against black people in America. While being appreciative of any support from any quarter in American society, including whites and other minorities, they are self-determined and not looking for the approval of whites to establish their agenda. The most important question for this discussion is, how will the church respond to this movement? How will the black church respond to this movement? What will we preach? Will we push deeper and deeper into these bigger subjects with real honesty and search for truth?

---

8. Rahiel Tefarmaiam, "Why the New Civil Rights Movement Keep Church Leaders at Arm's Length," *The Washington Post*, September 18, 2015, accessed November 16, 2016; available from www.washingtonpost.com/opinions/how-black-activism-lost-its-religion/2015/09/18/2f56fc00-5d6b-11e5-8e9e-dce8a2a2a679_story.html.

9. Simon Sebastian, "Don't Criticize Black Lives Matter for Provoking Violence. The Civil Rights Movement Did, Too," *The Washington Post*, October 1, 2015, accessed November 15, 2015; available from www.washingtonpost.com/posteverything/wp/2015/10/01/dont-criticize-black-lives-matter-for-provoking-violence-the-civil-rights-movement-did-too/.

In an article entitled "Why Black Lives Should Matter to the Church," Brittany Pashcall states, "Statistically, 87% of African Americans identify closely with a religious group. Similarly, 84% of Latin Americans identify closely with a religious group. This means that a large majority of those most frequently targeted for injustice occupy a pew on Sunday morning."[10]

As we said from the outset, more white Millennials, known as "nones" (those that check the "none" box when asked to state their religious affiliation), are leaving the church. Alan Bean, in an article entitled "Why (White) Millennials Are Leaving the Church," suggests that people of color comprise only one-third of American Millennials, and they represent over half of Millennial Christians.[11] Bean suggests that Millennials love the Jesus portrayed in the Bible, who preaches good news to the poor, and the upside-down kingdom, where "the first shall be last and the last shall be first." Bean suggests that Millennials "hear vague references to justice, caring for the poor, and feeding the hungry in many white churches, but the systematic roots of injustice, poverty and hunger are rarely explored."[12] Because most white churches find these teachings and their challenge to the core structures of American life to be so polemical in the congregation, they ignore as much of it as they can, or "ratchet up the machinery of denial," and frequently remain silent. The cognitive dissonance is too much for white Millennials, so they leave the church. Bean argues the black church is only slightly better since most minorities take the rough outlines of their theology from white Christians. What forces black churches to be slightly more political is that "bad public policy has such a devastating impact in poor communities of color."[13] He says, "There is just enough of the Jesus stuff in American's Black and Latino churches to sustain the commitment

---

10. Brittany Paschall, "Why Black Lives Should Matter to the Church," 2015, accessed October 21, 2015; available from http://unashamedimpact.com/blog/why-black-lives-should-matter-to-the-church.

11. Alan Bean, "Why (White) Millennials Are Leaving the Church," *Friends of Justice* (blog), accessed October 15, 2015; available from https://friendsofjustice.wordpress.com/2014/12/20/why-white-millennials-are-leaving-the-church.

12. Ibid.

13. Ibid.

of a restless millennial generation."[14] Frustrated by what they hear and see in their church community, there is enough social justice and a "dash of genuine Jesus-religion" to keep them coming.

Even though black Millennials are still coming, there are serious tensions between the black church and the new movement Millennials. Heretofore, the church has been the center of black America's struggle for civil rights. At the center of the black church has been traditional values, hierarchical male leadership, doctrinal opposition to the LGBTQ community, the politics of accommodation and respectability, and nonviolence and reconciliation. These traditional values are significant subjects that we must engage with real depth and honesty in order to find the truth. What is at stake in the church's response is if the black church is, or will ever be again, the main institution of black life and relevant to the needs and concerns of this new movement. Let us turn to the tension points more explicitly.

Tension Points: The New Movement and the Church

There are at least four principal tension points between the new movement and the church, the historical straight male leadership of the church, the disruptive tactics of the new movement, identification with and practice of black theology, and new movement proficiency with technology.

Tension One: The Historical Straight Male Leadership of the Church

For the most part, historically within the black church, women have been subordinated and restricted and the LGBTQ community has been ostracized and muted. The new movement demands the inclusion of women and the LGBTQ community as equal voices and partners. For example, women in the new movement predominately focused on violence against black men, until the death of Sandra Bland. As such, the hashtag #sayhername emerged, and the new movement addressed the is-

---

14. Ibid.

sue of full inclusion of the protest of police violence against women and girls, and also violence against transgender women. These key tenets of the new movement run counter to overwhelming belief of church doctrine on homosexuality, which many clergy and theologians believe is sin, and the almost lackluster inclusion of women in leadership and decision-making positions in church hierarchies.

The new movement does not rely upon a centralized charismatic leadership. That is, a single person, for example, who is accepted as the standard bearer of church leadership, whether that leader is female or male. Many in the new movement consider this model of leadership outdated. Those who operate out of this charismatic leadership model insist that the new movement appoint leaders, tone down the rhetoric, utilize less-confrontational tactics, and come to the negotiating table. If nothing else, history has taught the new movement that the standard-bearing leader can be assassinated and movements are severely debilitated. Besides the tactic of assassination, often in the charismatic sole leadership paradigm, black male preachers are co-opted and propped up as figureheads of those in political power. Often, they produce nothing for the black community other than their celebrity status, as evidenced by front seats at funerals, church, and sporting events; television coverage and shows; or their becoming the go-to authority on racial issues for the mainstream media. The new movement is clear about the kind of leadership they do not want. They do not want the church as the arbiter of the narrative of their emerging movement and have abandoned the church's model of leadership. Without change, the church runs the risk of being irrelevant to twenty-first-century political change.

Tension Two: Disruptive Tactics of the New Movement

While the church-based civil rights movement was anchored in nonviolent resistance strategies and moral suasion, the new movement is more confrontational, disrupting political rallies, sporting events, and shopping malls on holidays, not to mention morning and evening commutes. They are willing to "shut it down," with dispersed and hashtag organized protest movements around the country. Their model is not the Southern

Christian Leadership Council (SCLC), but rather the Black Panther Party. They openly declare, "Black power," wear natural hair, wave fists in the air, and come with clothing, apparel, signs, and symbols unapologetically announcing and celebrating blackness. The church, for the most part, has not been as radical in its rhetoric and tactics. Often for the church, black power has connotations of violence and separatism, and the church has operated from the sphere of accommodation, assimilation, negotiation, and change from within the power structures. What is more, the new movement is nonconciliatory and unapologetic about their righteous rage. They report that they have grown up disappointed with the gods of Generation X and the failure of political courage in the hip-hop generation. Their ultimate faith is in themselves to be agents of change, and admittedly they suggest that it might turn out to be hubris. But, what is clear, Tesfamariam says is that "they will not invest in a nation-state project that hands them black presidents alongside dead unarmed black boys in the street. These are irreconcilable contradictions. And these are non-conciliatory times."[15]

Tension Three: Identification with and Practice of Black Theology

From the perspective of the new movement, the church's deeply conservative theology and practice has led to a disconnection from social issues, and focus on personal success and affirmation, as suggested by the popular prosperity and celebrity preacher gospel doctrines, "get your blessing, breakthrough, and miracle theology." By and large, new movement young people ask, "What has happened to Jesus as a freedom fighter, liberator, community organizer, proclaimer of freedom from the captives, and revolutionary?" Where is the blending of substantive theology with real and astute political and economic critique?

Traditionally, our pulpit preaching has been freedom from sin, coupled with an aversion to homosexuality, affirmative of heteronormative male leadership, and Jesus as a life coach to help make you healthy, wealthy, and wise. Without any mention or challenge of structural issues such as systemic racism, police violence, income inequality or the like, listeners are taught to

---

15. Tesfamariam, "Why the Modern Civil Rights Movement Keep Religious Leaders at Arm's Length."

have good health, great relationships, and financial prosperity in family and business. Many churches employ a conservative theology of personal salvation that rarely addresses racism and structural oppression and liberation of the oppressed. This is not only white churches, but many black churches that accept the theological outlines of nonprophetic white theology.

Tension Four: Technological Proficiency of the New Movement

The new movement is diffuse, less centralized, and more collaborative because information is accessible to all and based upon the mobilizing force of social media. The world took notice of social media's ability to mobilize grassroots movements such as the Arab Spring and Occupy. The new movement is proving again what Todd Wolfson, author of *Digital Rebellion: The Birth of the Cyber Left*, said: "The Cyber Left is about flattening hierarchies, flattening governance processes, combined with using the logic of social networks for deep consensus building."[16]

Wolfson's comments are stark in regard to the new movement in that his statistics suggest that young, black Americans use social networking sites disproportionately. Ninety-six percent of African-American Internet users, aged eighteen to twenty-nine, use social networks of some kind. Forty percent of the same group say that they use Twitter—twelve percent more than the comparable figure for young white people.[17] Based upon young African Americans' increased social media usage, the social media emphasis of the new movement is effective in the creation of a liberation agenda. The mobilizing force of social media means that the new movement is not linked by physical proximity or political consensus or platforms, and yet there is a strength in dispersion. Heretofore, what could be ignored by the time delay of broadcasts or the agenda of the media cannot now be ignored:

> A hashtag on Twitter can link the disparate fates of unarmed black men shot down by white police in a way that transcends geographical boundaries and time zones. A shared post on Facebook can organize a protest

---

16. Elizabeth Day, "#BlackLivesMatter: The Birth of a New Civil Rights Movement," *The Guardian*, July 15, 2015, accessed December 3, 2015; available from www.theguardian.com/world/2015/jul/19/blacklivesmatter-birth-civil-rights-movement#img-2.

17. Ibid.

in a matter of minutes. Documentary photos and videos can be distributed on Tumblr pages and Periscope feeds, through Instagrams and Vines. Power lies in a single image.[18]

Through the use of social media, the new movement is quick and adept in shaping its own narrative. While national media, including newspapers, editorials, op-eds, blogs, and cable news and their pundits have their own viewpoints, new movement people are on the scene sharing their perspectives on social media, often presenting a very different picture. Instantly the movement can write its own story anywhere, anytime. One of the ways these different perspectives can play out in the relationship between the church and the new movement is majorities of older church communities are more dependent on traditional national and cable media outlets for information and perspectives, while those in the new movement create and shape their own narrative of events. Sometimes the church and the new movement can have two different narratives of the same event based upon their source of information.

Are religious institutions, inclusive of denominations and seminaries, relevant to these organizations? How relevant is preaching in black churches to this movement? And, if a preacher wanted to be relevant to this movement, how and what would the preacher preach?

THE CHURCH AND THE NEW MOVEMENT

Now that we have established the bigger subjects that require real depth and honesty, I want to discuss the aforementioned four areas of tension in regard to the church and its relevance to preaching. What is at stake is if the black church is, or will ever be again, the main institution of black life and relevant to the concerns of all of its constituency groups. Our main goal is truth, because as Jay-Z claims, truth is always relevant. Let's start with a discussion of the tension of black theology and disruptive tactics.

Black Theology and Disruptive Tactics

There are churches that the new movement mentions as relevant in their own writing about their movement, ministries like First Corinthian

---

18. Ibid.

Baptist in New York City (Harlem), City of Refuge United Church of Christ in Oakland, California, and Community of Hope AME in Temple Hills, Maryland. There are many more around the country that are dedicated to the liberation-centered legacy of the black church, such as Trinity United Church of Christ and St. Sabina Catholic in Chicago, Illinois, Samuel DeWitt Proctor Conference, Inc., to name a few. There are numerous churches that are rooted in black liberation theology, and fiercely believe that the church is a tool for the empowerment of the oppressed. Jesus, for these churches, is a freedom fighter, liberator, revolutionary, and challenger of the status quo. Churches such as these participate in the new movement in various ways, such as "Hoodie Sunday" when Trayvon Martin was killed, "die-in" marches, shouting, "I can't breathe," following the death of Eric Garner, and the "Seven Last Words" services of black people killed by police. Several churches opened their doors to tear gas victims and served as sanctuary in Ferguson and Baltimore when conflict escalated between protesters and police. Clergy, in both cities, organized themselves, and held protest meetings in their churches and asked their members to participate in protest marches and support. In sum, these churches are connected in visceral and tangible action-oriented ways to the agenda and resolve of the new movement. Outside of times of acute crisis, many churches participate daily in acts of mercy and kindness (i.e., food banks, clothes closets, training centers for GED education) and opposition to structural discrimination and shortsighted social policy such as "Souls to the Polls," voter registration drives, and others. And generally, we can conclude that if congregational support is happening for these activities, it is a reflection of the effective and relevant sermons preached from the pulpit. These preachers are preaching about these issues effectively and are inspiring their people into action.

While all of the above is true, the new movement is speaking prophetically and challenging the black church, pointing toward its silence on issues such as mass incarceration, urban gun violence, health and food deserts, and disparities of services in low income neighborhoods. Factually, there are numerous churches that support the new movement, however only a small number of churches are engaged in direct protest of issues of social justice. The same was true in the 1950s and 1960s. Then, only a small minority adopted the civil rights movement agenda. The new movement speaks prophetically and challenges the church's lack of response to organized, structural, and systemic racial inequality in black neighborhoods. Many churches, if they address the issues at all, play it safe.

For young people of the new movement, playing it safe means that, for example, churches speak to issues of militarized policing in black neighborhoods, but the goal is to placate, that is, affirm the sense of injustice, and disaffirm their right to certain kinds of acts of righteous rage at the injustice itself. Playing it safe are comments from many pulpits, ideas in meetings, messages in sermons, requests in the media, and practices that ask the new movement to turn down its rage. In truth, white America is, and has always been, afraid and paranoid of black rage, and so is the respectable and conservative black church. From the perspective of the new movement, the goal of playing safe is to allow the protesters to "let off steam," offer prayers over them, and then send them home in order to keep the false peace.

The church has difficulty with the rage of the new movement, just as the church has difficulty with the rage of Jesus in Matthew 21:2 and John 2:15. Jesus cleans the temple of moneychangers based on righteous rage and indignation. The church is not comfortable with the rage of Jesus, and the rage in poor communities that often produces burning of buildings, violent language, disruption of business property, and the flow of commerce. It is possible to understand, sympathize, and feel oneself the rage, and not condone the violence that rage can produce. This is the tension the church finds itself in: often willing to temper the rage that burns and does violence, and rightfully so, but without forceful, meaningful, and creative solutions to address the issues. While not condoning violence, King said that riots are the language of the unheard and offered viable alternatives to violence.[19] He did not condone rage and the violence, but he understood it. Does the church understand it? Speaking to a group of international teachers of preaching, South African professor Johan Cilliers

---

19. "MLK: A Riot Is the Language of the Unheard," August 25, 2015. Based upon Mike Wallace's interview with Martin Luther King Jr., September 27, 1966, for CBS News, accessed February 5, 2015, at www.cbsnews.com/news/mlk-a-riot-is-the-language-of-the-unheard/.

quotes Walter Brueggemann, in calling for a *theology of anger*: "Preaching that expresses this *pro-vocare*, this provocation may and should sometimes be born out of a *theology of anger*. This theology of anger cries out in God's name that things cannot continue as they are." Speaking of the preaching of prophets in South Africa, Cilliers says, "We have been blessed in this country with preaching who practiced and still practice, *this theology of indignation, of interruption and holy provocation*"[20] (emphasis added). Does the church try to understand it? Does the church have viable and creative alternatives? Can the church understand the new movement and its rage when it says that a nation that does not protect its citizens should no longer be surprised when the citizens no longer believe in the idea of the nation itself? Can the church grapple with, confront, and understand, and in some shape or form adopt a prophetic, compassionate, truth-telling and hopeful theology of anger?

I believe that every preacher who seeks to understand and work with creative solutions should read Patrick Sharkey's *Stuck in Place: Urban Neighborhoods and the End of the Progress toward Racial Equality*.[21] While researchers typically analyze the economic inequality/mobility of racial/ethnic groups by focusing on individual factors such as the home, family structure, human capital, or culture as affecting character, Sharkey rightly looks beyond the individual and the family to understand inequality/mobility in regards to the importance of place, that is, communities and neighborhoods as sites for the transmission of racial inequality in the post–civil rights era. He believes that inequality is organized in and around space.

Sharkey argues the problem of urban poverty is not only that concentrated poverty has intensified and racial segregation has persisted, but the same families have experienced the consequences of living in disadvantaged neighborhoods over multiple generations. The ghetto is inherited. The problems and challenges of the urban ghetto have been

---

20. Delivered at the twelfth biannual conference of the *Societas Homiletica*, held in Stellenbosch, South Africa, March 11–16, 2016, on the theme "Preaching Promise within the Paradoxes of Life."

21. Patrick Sharkey, *Stuck in Place: Urban Neighborhoods and the End of the Progress toward Racial Equality* (Chicago: The University of Chicago Press, 2013).

experienced, and then passed on to children, which means for generations families have experienced the nation's worst schools and most unhealthy and violent environments. He, for example, argues that white and black children are raised in entirely distinct environments. From the 1950s to 1970s 4 percent of whites were raised in neighborhoods with at least 20 percent poverty compared to 62 percent of African Americans. During 1985 to 2000, it got even worse, with two out of three black children raised in neighborhoods with 20 percent poverty compared to 6 percent of whites. It is devastating when 66 percent of African American children grow up in neighborhoods with at least 20 percent poverty and 31 percent of African American children live in neighborhoods with a poverty rate at 30 percent, poverty rates unknown among white children. When one lives in a high poverty neighborhood that is economically depressed and therefore unhealthy and safe, there are few opportunities for mobility and success.[22] Whites and blacks group up in different neighborhoods and environments and have different experiences and therefore different experiences of America. Many call the experience of the majority of white Americans in these different neighborhoods, "white privilege."

Concentrations of violence go hand in hand with concentrations of poverty. Through extant maps of homicides in the city of Chicago, Sharkey demonstrates that entire sections of the city never know the most extreme form of violence, a local homicide. There are other neighborhoods where homicides are normative. This is not the result of character deficiencies of poor families. Instead it is because areas composed of primarily poor racial and ethnic minorities have been objects of severe disinvestment and abandonment for the most part of the past half century. What is more, Sharkey correctly contends:

> If segregated neighborhoods with concentrated poverty had greater levels of political influence, amenities that are taken for granted in middle-class communities, quality public services and schools, a vibrant economic base, and effective policing, then segregation and the concentration of poverty would decline and would not necessarily be associated with gang activity, crime, and violence, teenage childbearing and high dropout

---

22. Ibid., 27–28.

rates, poor community health, joblessness, homelessness, and blight. The social problems that are prevalent in America's ghettoes are the product of shortsighted policies, intentional efforts to isolate or exclude minority communities within cities, and major economic and demographic shifts.[23]

Again, he makes the point that these problems are not the result of character deficiencies and deficits among the urban poor. Rather there is systemic and societal neglect that makes the ghetto possible and even convenient. Can the church preach about this? Can we understand? I do not condone violence that is often the result of rage, but I do understand. Do we have creative solutions? This is the truth: we have abandoned certain neighborhoods and families, and then are surprised when they respond with destructive rage. Our ignorance and innocence is alarming when we make the announcement that "we do not understand why they are burning their own neighborhoods." Admittedly, there is a criminal element made up of destructive fools who take advantage of the opportunity to loot and make mayhem, but the majority of the people want what middle-class neighborhoods want—quality public services and schools, effective policing, jobs and a vibrant economic base, and because no one has heard their cry, they respond with violence and rage.

And the question is: Does understanding this lead to creative, positive, and constructive involvement and action by the church? For the new movement, if preaching does not lead to concrete action, then that preaching is safe. If the purpose of preaching is to support and sanction a blessed personal life within the context of the status quo, an unequal and flawed social and economic system, then that preaching is safe and not acceptable to this new movement. Millennials are seeking substantive theological reflection balanced by honest and true social critique that leads to engagement by the church and its leaders. They are looking for creative action and not safe words.

I am not condemning churches and suggesting that every church should preach black liberation theology, and that if churches are not involved in the new movement, they are not the church. My goal is not to fill

---

23. Ibid.

this chapter with criticism based upon "shoulds," "oughts," and "musts," such that people are manipulated out of inactivity. What I am suggesting is that if you want to be relevant to these young people, then at the very minimum the preacher must preach and be honest about the rage. We must preach and offer critical theological reflection around Jesus throwing the moneychangers from the temple and passages that are supported by insightful social critique. If you want to reach these young people, you must find what is just in their cause and be honest about it.

It starts at the deepest levels of belief and conviction within each person. It takes honest self-reflection from each person to look at the ways in which they are complicit, that is, blissfully ignorant, naively innocent, callously indifferent, or willingly neglectful, and then engage self into the issues. The purpose here is not to lay guilt trips on anyone and assert what every Christian and every black church should be doing. The worst thing in the world is to preach about such issues without accurate information and analysis and some level of deep inner clarity and moral conviction. To preach about these issues out of ignorance and innocence is to do harm to oneself, one's congregation, and the new movement. If one is prepared with accurate analysis, inner clarity, and moral conviction, one is prepared when one's preaching becomes controversial in many places. If one preaches about it, it will not make everyone comfortable. If one preaches about it, one will be called unflattering names and some will not want to hear a word of it. To preach about it and couple it with effective action is to go against the grain of apathy and conformism and swim upstream against the tide of conservatism in the church.

Some preachers and congregations are ready and poised for a social action agenda of systemic critique and mass protests. I would like to make a few comments to those who are not ready and are in some kind of process to possibly get ready. In this circumstance, if you are going to preach about these issues, invite dialogue before and after the sermon, particularly if you think it is going to be controversial. Before the sermon, it might be possible to meet with Millennials in the church and those in the new movement, and dialogue with them. Bishop Joseph W. Walker III has an MAT (Millennial Advisory Team) that he meets with for ongoing discussion and input.[24] He describes the meetings as invaluable, as they give input and tremendous suggestions to aid and assist his preaching. It is possible to be collaborative in the development of the sermon. Several doctor of ministry preaching programs in the country teach and advocate that laypeople be assembled and partner with preachers in the development and preaching of the sermon.

In my pastoring experience, I have learned the hard way of taking controversial positions in sermons without the requisite amount of preparation of the people. I made statements and took positions that I had not prepared the people for. Many people would have been helped to receive my positions had I prepared the people with dialogue, information, and training. There are no guarantees and many have found with preparation, information, and training certain people make their opposition known in harmful and divisive ways. Dialogue, training, and information does not do away with opposition; it simply gives the preacher's position the best chance to receive and illicit thoughtful response in support or opposition.

It is only in "fierce" dialogue that the hard questions can get raised and heard. I mean the term *fierce* in the way mentioned in the acknowledgments, where we come from behind ourselves and say something that is honestly and profoundly true for us and then also hear what is profoundly true for others. When the environment is fierce, hard questions can be asked. The new movement can ask the church hard questions about its conservative ideology, its silence, and therefore its complicity in the systemic oppression of people. The church will ask the new movement why they march and protest and create mass movements when officers shoot unarmed black people but then are relatively silent around the vast levels of black-on-black murder and gun violence in the black community. I know that this is an oft-mentioned talking point to divert the discussion from the reality of racism and police brutality. But there is some truth in this question that the church and the new movement must address. In Jay-Z's terms, these are the big subjects, and it is possible that when we have a fierce conversation where we listen to and speak what is profoundly

---

24. For more information, see "Presiding Bishop Joseph W. Walker III," www.fullgospelbaptist.org/bishop-joseph-w-walkers-biography/.

true for each of us, understanding and dialogue can happen, and change is possible.

In the new movement, there is a different leadership model, one based upon the inclusion of women and the LGBTQ community. The truth is that leadership styles can be generational and the leadership style of the new movement is much more collaborative than leadership styles of the past. The black church must come to the table as a collaborator, as an equal with all others, willing to learn, teach, listen, and speak. If the church, because of its traditional role of leadership, attempts to exert control and dominance, then the church will find itself the only voice at the table. If the church tries to seize the mic, the agenda, and the publicity with celebrity preachers, young people will interrupt and disrupt the agenda.[25] In truth, if the church presses its doctrinal position in terms of homosexuals and women as a litmus test of who can be included in the conversation and who can exert leadership, then, at least for the new movement, the church will not be relevant.

What the church must do is learn the value of coalition building and working with people even if there is disagreement for a greater goal. I recently went to a production entitled *April 4, 1968* and heard this phrase: "We disagree on the same side." What is important is not that we agree on every doctrine or tactic, but that we are on the same side. The vast array of the tools of systemic oppression requires coalitions to address issues and concerns. There is no one group, church, or generation that will defeat these forces in and of themselves. Coalitions must be built, despite differences of opinions, in matters of doctrine, style and taste, and even tactics. There are congregations that openly affirm homosexuality and others that do not, but what is true is that the church must be inclusive with others who have the same community interest at heart. There is always a faith-filled minority, which has leaned into the moment of movements of social justice, and the determination of those who participate has never been based upon gender and sexual preference. Though there were issues of

---

25. See Matt Laslo, "Al Sharpton Is Struggling to Control the 'Black Lives Matter' Movement," *Vice*, December 18, 2014, accessed December 1, 2015; available from www.vice.com/read/al-sharpton-is-struggling-to-control-the-black-lives-matter-movement-1218.

gender and inclusion of homosexual people in the civil rights movement, the new movement simply makes explicit this truth: come as you are.

Finally, it is no secret that the church lags behind in methodologies of social media. The issue is so obvious that it is not necessary to spend much time on it other than to suggest that the church not adopt the methodologies without understanding how they have changed communication. As we said before, social media flattens hierarchies, flattens governance processes, and builds deep consensus. Anyone can send a text and post a message to be hip and "keep up with the young people"; the real issue is how to share information with transparency and build consensus for movement. Many churches use social media to brand themselves and connect with audiences, members, and others who value the ministry offerings. Churches use it to build consensus among the members and potential member audiences. The question is: Can the church use its present social media networks to build consensus in the interest of building movements to help the community gain access to quality public services and schools, effective policing, jobs and a vibrant economic base?

Taking the Long View

In the concluding section of this chapter, I want to take the long view and offer suggestions as to how the church can offer further value to the new movement. My hope is that this discussion has created a level of understanding such that Millennials would find their voice heard in a church community. In truth, a partnership is needed that involves the creative energy and bold determinism of young people and the wisdom, experience, and longevity of the older crowd. There are many lessons that the church can learn from the new movement, and likewise numerous lessons that the new movement can learn from longevity and historical sweep of the black struggle for freedom and justice in America. The black community has pushed deeper and deeper into the biggest subjects of racism, violence, and oppression for generations and learned truths that are relevant for every generation. As Jay-Z says, the truth is always relevant.

One truth is that racism and oppression is deeply embedded in the American experiment. History has taught that each time blacks have made strides for freedom, there has been backlash, retrenchment, and new forms of subjugation that appear on the American landscape, thus the old oppression in a new guise. The new movement is part of a long historical sweep, and it has taken many lifetimes to get to this point in the struggle. Because of the tenacity of opposition to equality of race and economics in America, we cannot "throw the baby out with the bathwater" by looking upon past struggles and tradition with disdain. Past struggles have involved sacrifices and deaths to make possible the dignity and respect of African American people. How many sacrifices and what deaths will it take in the new movement, in the words of King, to "make America what it ought to be"? The truth that is relevant is that we honor those in any generation who sacrifice and lay down their lives for freedom. We do not yet know what will be required of any of us in this march to freedom.

Another truth that is always relevant is that social justice movements must be deeply connected with sources of spiritual enrichment and vitality. The prolific mystic and social justice advocate Howard Thurman suggests that he noticed, particularly in those people who work for social justice and improving social conditions, a kind of despair. He said that many activists recognized that what they were doing was good, true, and significant, but they were working against the way things fundamentally were in human life, and it caused in them a kind of despair. Human beings are, for example, fundamentally selfish, and to improve things, people are asked through moral suasion to be unselfish, to be concerned about someone outside their group, persons they would not normally consider their sisters and brothers. For many people, only the people of their kind or their group are their brothers and sisters. And even if the liberation appeal is not to moral suasion, but demands for equality made from the power politics of voting numbers, protest marches, and economic strength through boycotts, and so forth, still the entrenched forces of opposition mutate and find ways to maneuver such to co-opt the movement and the progress made. For those who love freedom and justice, there is the glory of victory that makes change and the agony of defeat that no matter what changes things stay the same. Those who work for justice come to know the depth of the reality of human nature and the entrenchment of forces against freedom and justice. Thurman was aware of this truth and labeled it a susceptibility to despair.

The truth that is always relevant is in the face of such potential for despair; spiritual resources are needed to escape the fall into cynicism and radical violence. The new movement is finding and creating its own spiritual resources. For example, though anthems for Millennials tend to change quickly, some speculate that the new black national anthem for black Millennials is Kendrick Lamar's "Alright." During a Black Lives Matter protest in Cleveland, protesters were chanting lyrics from "Alright": "We gon' be alright! We gon' be alright."[26] Aisha Harris says about "Alright":

> The chorus is simple yet extraordinarily intoxicating, easy to chant, offering a kind of comfort that people of color and other oppressed communities desperately need all too often: the hope—the feeling—that despite tensions in this country growing worse and worse, in the long run, we're all gon' be all right. And more than that—the specific kind of comfort that comes from repeating that line over and over.[27]

"We gon' be alright! We gon' be alright." Harris says that she listens to the song because "the world seems like a terrible place." Hearing the news of another black person shot by police, a young girl's birthday party turns into an unnecessarily horrifying police encounter. A white supremacist murders black church members during a prayer session? She says she in each instance turns on "Alright." "We gon' be alright! We gon' be alright." The truth is the church and the older generation knows repeating sounds, songs, and phrases that give hope in seemingly hopeless situations. The truth is that chants of Lamar's lyrics sound like a remix of "We Shall Overcome" and our discussion of Gardner C. Taylor's "It's Alright Now," from chapter 3.

26. "Kendrick Lamar's 'Alright' Changed by Protesters during Cleveland Altercation," Jeremy Gordon, *Pitchfork*, July 29, 2015, http://pitchfork.com/news/60568-kendrick-lamars-alright-chanted-by-protesters-during-cleveland-police-altercation/.

27. Aisha Harris, "Has Kendrick Lamar Recorded the New Black National Anthem? Singing 'Alright' in a Summer of Protest, Despair, and Hope," 2015, accessed November 20, 2015; available from *Slate*, www.slate.com/articles/arts/culturebox/2015/08/black_lives_matter_protesters_chant_kendrick_lamar_s_alright_what_makes.html.

CHAPTER FIVE

Actually the full lyrics are: "But if God got us—Then we gon' be alright." Reports are that Kendrick Lamar is a Christian and several of his songs have Christian lyrics. Maybe in a very different way, through hip-hop gospel, the church is providing spiritual resources of hope to those who struggle for a new world. I believe the church can be relevant if it pushes deeper and deeper into the bigger subjects with real honesty. When we deal with the truth, Millennials and the church will find they have a tremendous amount in common. I thank God for Kendrick Lamar and the churches that are relevant to the new movement, and I also have not given up on the traditional church in all of its conservative ideology. The truth is always relevant. "We gon' be alright! We gon' be alright!"

Afterword
"SEVEN DECADES OF AFRICAN AMERICAN PREACHING"

by Jeremiah A. Wright Jr.

Delivered at Christian Theological Seminary

Indianapolis, Indiana

March 4, 2015

Video available at www.youtube.com/watch?v=3R3Jchy5M_Y1

When asked to share my thoughts and perspectives on black preaching by one of the premiere professors and practitioners of homiletics in the nation, I asked myself what could I possibly bring to the table in a discussion about preaching, where the Academy of Preaching and Celebration is housed, where seminarians have access to consultations on African American preaching, and to Frank A. Thomas, one of the world's leading experts on preaching? It sounded like I would be taking sand to the beach to talk about preaching in a place where Frank A. Thomas teaches preaching.

Then, after praying about the matter, God showed me that sharing what I have seen in seven decades when it comes to preaching in the context of the portion of the black religious experience that I have experienced would be of value to some seminarian preparing herself for a life

---

1. Readers might also be interested in Frank A. Thomas interviewing Jeremiah A. Wright Jr., "On Preaching," https://www.youtube.com/watch?v=qRq-kXWJ80U.

of service to the church of Jesus Christ, or preparing himself to pastor a people where preaching forty-eight to fifty times a year for twenty to thirty years seems like an impossible task.

I want to talk to you, therefore, about what I have seen, what I have heard, and what and whom I have experienced in seven decades of being a product of and a practitioner of black preaching in the context of the United States iteration of the North American black Atlantic Diaspora.

In trying to frame my presentation and in trying to condense or summarize seven decades, I had to come to grips with my perspective on black preaching being shaped by the foundational formation of the school of theology at Virginia Union University. Before I outline to you what I have seen and heard in black preaching for seven decades, allow me to share the formations and foundations of my preaching.

My grandfather, Rev. Hamilton Martin Henderson, was a product of Virginia Union University. It was in the churches he pastored that I heard the foundational aspects and understandings of "Virginia Union homiletics." I was carried to and worshipped in the rural churches he pastored from the time I was born and carried down south for holidays, vacations, or the summer, from infancy until I was in the seventh grade, and my maternal grandparents moved into a home in Philadelphia.

My grandfather was a product of the school of theology at Virginia Union University. My grandfather's perspective and his point of departure when it came to preaching in a country—not rural—but a "country" black church, was shaped by the peculiarity of what Cornel West calls "the hybridity of Diasporic African existence." Cornel West and I co-led a doctor of ministry group at United Theological Seminary back in the 1980s, and in one of his lectures to our class, Dr. West called the African American Diasporic experience in the Black Atlantic a classic example of European-African-European American and African American "hybridity." A hybrid culture was created in the Black Atlantic. My grandfather was a product of Euro-centric theological education while serving a black congregation in the "deep" country (backwoods) of Virginia.

My grandfather was a phenomenon. He was not let off of the plantation on which he was born until the age of twenty. And at the age of twenty, he had no education whatsoever. Born in Henderson, North Carolina, he was raised in a cultural climate with a long history of racist thought, racist teaching, and racist practices, a state where it had been against the law to teach an African to read. At the age of twenty, he had never seen the inside of a school or a book, but he started school at the age of twenty anyhow. He finished grammar school, high school, and college at Virginia Union. He graduated from college, and graduated from Virginia Union Seminary in 1902. His diploma hangs on my wall in my study. My grandfather was a product of the school of theology at Virginia Union University.

His perspective as a black preacher was forged in the frames of North Carolina racism, and refined in the classrooms of northern white missionaries who came south to teach at the schools set up for the Freedmen (hybridity). With two degrees, he chose to stay in the South to teach at a two-room school to give some other black boys and girls in Virginia an education, an opportunity to go further than the farm, and a vision of what was possible when one used the mind God gave them, and refused to be defined by others who saw them as less than human. He taught in that two-room school while pastoring the Gravel Hill Baptist Church in Surry County, Virginia, for twenty years, and then pastoring Jerusalem Baptist Church in Temperanceville, Virginia, on the eastern shore of Virginia for another fifteen years before moving, as I said, into our home in Philadelphia, when I was in the seventh grade.

The black preaching I heard in his churches was shaped by the peculiarity of "the hybridity of Diasporic African existence." In other words, it was neither pure European nor European American. Nor was it pure African or African American. It was a "mixture" or what Gayraud Wilmore calls in his *Black Religion and Black Radicalism*, "a *tertium quid*."[2] My grandfather was a grandson of Africans who were enslaved, son of a black woman whose parents knew the whip of the overseer, and shaped also by northern missionaries who taught European and British culture as being synonymous with Christianity. (Hybridity.)

---

2. Gayraud S. Wilmore, *Black Religion and Black Radicalism: An Interpretation of the Religious History of African Americans* (Maryknoll, NY: Orbis Books, 1998), 14.

The black preaching I heard from his children also had a Virginia Union University foundation. One of his sons, John Bennett Henderson, pastored the Bank Street Baptist Church in Norfolk, Virginia, where Samuel DeWitt Proctor was a member, and where Proctor's family still belongs. John Henderson graduated from Virginia Union University and earned his master of divinity from Oberlin—a school with a long track record of antislavery activity and the education of African Americans (complex hybridity): and he pastored in the segregated south, Norfolk, Virginia.

Not only my grandfather's son, his daughter, my mother, was a graduate of Virginia Union University. A preacher not called a "preacher" in the 1940s, 1950s, 1960s, or 1970s because she was a woman. Called a minister; called a women's day speaker; but a black preacher nevertheless. And, an educated one with one master's degree from the University of Chicago; a second master's from the University of Pennsylvania and her terminal degree also from the University of Pennsylvania. A black preacher who knew racism up close and personal, but whose Virginia Union perspective combined with her rural Virginia upbringing gave her the foundation on which I stand.

One sidebar—in fact two sidebars—my mother taught me this. She said I had a close friend who was a Catholic. We were neighbors who grew up together, Vincent Richardson and I. We were trying to understand each other's faith traditions. As a Roman Catholic, he couldn't eat fish on Friday, and started crying in summer camp because we had hot dogs on Friday. He would come to my church and didn't understand people raising their hands. So, to make us feel better my mother told this story. She said:

> Two little boys just like you decided the best way to learn each other's faith was to go to church with each other. So, the Catholic boy said, "You come to my church first." And he explained genuflection. He explained the sign of the cross—Father, Son, and Holy Ghost. He explained Communion, and the Mass. Then they went to the Baptist church, and the Baptist kid was explaining to his Catholic friend why people kept interrupting the preacher. Why they really weren't waving at anybody. And then when the preacher stood up to preach, he took off

his watch and the little Baptist boy didn't say anything. So his Catholic friend asked, "What does that mean?" He said, "Not a damn thing."

My mother as a woman preacher blessed my life. My second year of pastoring, I called home one Sunday afternoon after I had flunked. "Flunking" in the black preaching tradition is when the dialogical nature of the preaching moment does not occur as anticipated by the preacher. The sermon in a dialogue in the black church is not a monologue. When, therefore, a climactic dialogue does not happen, the preacher is said to have "flunked." It was my first time flunking as a pastor and my mother answered the phone. And I said, "Is Daddy home?" And she said, "No, he's in an afternoon service." I said, "Okay, I'll call him back." She said, "What's wrong with you?" I said, "I need to talk to Daddy." She said, "Why do you need to talk to Daddy and you can't talk to me?" I replied, "I need to talk to a preacher." She said, "Oh, it's going to be like that, huh?" I said, "No, no, no, no; I mean I need to talk to one who preaches every Sunday." She said, "Well, I don't preach every Sunday, but my husband is a preacher who preaches every Sunday, my brother's a preacher who preaches every Sunday, my father was a preacher." I said, "Mommy, do you know what flunk is?" She said, "Every preacher knows what flunk is. Don't you remember I told you when I went to Charles Booth's church what happened to me? Flunk was on the same plane riding in first class. When I got up that morning, he got up earlier. He was in the presidential suite in the hotel. He went to the church and waited on me at the pulpit. When I stood up to preach he said, 'Come here.' Don't you remember that?" I said, "Yes ma'am." But, my father taught me, and we used to call each other every Saturday night. "Are you Ghost-ed up for tomorrow?" My father taught me that if the Holy Ghost don't meet you in the study, don't look for him in the pulpit. No need of you talking about, "Help me, Holy Ghost." It's too late! He wanted to help you in the preparation—not just in the proclamation! The Holy Ghost wants to meet you in the study!" I said to my mother, "Well, I met the Holy Ghost. We had this thing together. I thought it was uptight and it flunked. That's what's wrong."

AFTERWORD

My mother said to me, "Do you aspire to be a master at the craft of preaching? Be honest." I said, "Yes ma'am." She said, "That is a noble aspiration. Don't ever give up on it and don't ever think you've made it. But, while you continue to strive to be a master at your craft of preaching, please remember this. Every piece by a master is not a masterpiece. You see the ones that made it to the museum. You don't see the ones at home and in the attic. Your members get to see the stuff at home, but they love you so don't worry about it. Remember the batting averages of Babe Ruth and Hank Aaron. When a pro has a batting average of .300 or even .400, that means they struck out six or seven times out of ten times at bat! You're not going to knock it out of the park every time."

That's the foundation—half the foundation I should say, because my father was also a graduate of Virginia Union University. My father earned a bachelor of theology, a bachelor of arts, and a master of divinity from Virginia Union. His experiences growing up in the segregated south of Caroline County, Virginia, were blended with the missionary teachings of an HBCU (Historically Black College and University) also as he pastored the Grace Baptist Church of Germantown in Philadelphia, Pennsylvania, for forty-two years. Thus, the black preaching I heard from the pulpit where my daddy served also became the framework through which I heard, understood, evaluated, critiqued, enjoyed, endured, and accepted and/or rejected black preaching.

With that as my background, let's talk about seventy years of black preaching.

I'm going to call names that you probably don't know. You can study the names I will call, Google them, and find out who these persons are because our worlds are two different worlds—the black religious experience and the non–African American religious institution, Christian Theological Seminary.

My exposure to and understanding of black preaching was in the context of my experiences in Philadelphia and Virginia from the age of three until the age of thirteen, with my dad being a part then of the National Baptist Convention, the Lott Carey Convention, and the Hampton Ministers' Conference, and my mom being a part of the International

Ministers' Wives and Widows Association. They would drag me to all of those meetings. I heard my first non–seminary-trained pastor at a National Baptist Convention in Philadelphia that will forever be a part of my memories.

The National Baptist Convention was meeting in Convention Hall in Philadelphia. And back in those days they had wooden folding chairs and all the preachers wore straw hats. Some were flat top; some parted down the middle. And C. L. Franklin preached on growing old in this land. C. L. Franklin never made it to seminary. C. L. Franklin spent ninety to nine-five seconds on growing old and what growing old was like. He spent ninety seconds on in this land, and this was in 1953, the year before the Supreme Court's ruling on desegregation, where he talked about being segregated from the cradle through the cemetery—segregated hospitals, segregated nurseries, and segregated cemeteries. He came back on ninety more seconds on growing old; ninety seconds on in this land; what it was like in this land with the Scottsboro boys and so on. About eighteen or twenty minutes into his sermon, he shifted gears and he said (in cadence and tune): "But-er-rum, there is a land, oh Lord-er-rum. There is a land where we will never, never," and when he reached the third "never," Aretha [Franklin], his daughter, stood up and in that same key started singing "Never Grow Old." Chairs were flying, hats were off—this was my exposure to and understanding of black preaching.

I heard seminary-trained black preachers in those formative years, like John Malcus Ellison, who was taught by the missionaries that you don't show any emotion in preaching—never. Samuel DeWitt Proctor, whose dialectical method of preaching became a part of my staple, sermon preparation, my way of doing exegesis and my hermeneutic when looking at the scriptures and preparing a sermon. Dr. Proctor used to teach me and drummed into my head, not in this first decade, but while I was at Virginia Union, where he was the president in 1959 and 1960. With just the two of us driving in his car on our trips back and forth up to Philadelphia from Richmond, Virginia, we would practice his dialectical method.

Gardner C. Taylor was my father's close friend—Sandy Ray, Howard Thurman, my daddy's black road dog—J. Quentin Jackson, pastor of the

Mt. Zion Baptist Church, and my daddy's white friend—V. Carney Hargroves, pastor of the Second Baptist Church of Germantown, who used to come to our black congregation and preach. He was a white pastor, and he was my sister's and my direct contact to Santa Claus. We took our Santa Claus letters to Dr. Hargroves because we knew he was white and Santa was white. Daddy told us that Rev. Hargroves knew Santa Claus personally.

I heard seminary-trained preaching and non–seminary-trained preaching in the same decade of my life down at St. John Baptist Church in Caroline County, Virginia. I heard Sunday afternoon preaching. Sunday afternoon services, one hundred degrees, windows open, food smells coming through the window, this one man stood up and preached on the Twenty-Third Psalm. He couldn't spell *seminary*. He started off with *the*—first word in the Lord's Twenty-Third Psalm. That's a definite article as opposed to an indefinite article. *It's not a Lord; it's The Lord.* And he spent a few seconds on *The Lord is*. Then he came back for three more minutes on *The Lord is my*. By the time he got down to *surely goodness and mercy*, you couldn't hear him. They were making more noise in the church than he was in his preaching. Powerfully packed together: theology from the folk and not theology from seminary in that same decade.

In the second decade, from the age of fourteen to twenty-four, my exposure to and understanding of black preaching was in the context of my daddy leaving the National Baptist Convention, in 1961, the year the man got killed in Kansas City, and taking our church into the American Baptist Convention. In this second decade, I graduated from Central High School in Philadelphia and went to Virginia Union in Richmond. I was part of the sit-ins at Virginia Union University, where my white Christian friends, who shared the word of God with me from Richmond Polytechnic Institute, which is now Virginia Commonwealth University, in the context of the Christian college clubs, were calling me "nigger" in the context of the sit-ins. In this decade, I had two years in the United States Marine Corps and four years in the United States Navy. I also heard a wide variety of black preaching in my second decade of being a part of a black religious tradition.

"Seven Decades of African American Preaching"

While a student at Virginia Union University, I heard Samuel DeWitt Proctor, Allix B. James, Howard Chubbs, and Paul Martin, who is now president of American Baptist Seminary of the West. I heard E. D. McCreary, who was a ThD, earned doctorate, and taught both undergraduate and seminary at Virginia Union Seminary and pastored in Richmond, Virginia. He was both a professor and a pastor. I heard Gordon Blaine Hancock, with his doctorate from Harvard University, who taught both of my parents, and who taught black economics teaching Christians about, what he called, the "double duty dollar." He would say, "Make your dollar do double duty. Stop earning your money and spending it in the white community; spend it in the black community. Why do you spend your money at stores where you can't try on your clothes?" This was in the 1930s. Most of us who had no cars walked to his church on Sundays. His nephew, whom he also sent to Harvard University, would come into Richmond and preach also. Dr. Hancock's nephew was none other than Charles G. Adams (aka The Harvard Hooper). I heard Morris Wellington Lee, and I heard the pastors of the Fifth Street Baptist Church and the Fifth Baptist Church of Richmond. Because our choir at Virginia Union would go to different churches to raise money, I got to hear preaching from all of those Virginia Union pastors in the city of Richmond, Virginia, and surrounding townships.

I got to hear Martin Luther King Jr. while in college. I got to hear Adam Clayton Powell Jr. I heard my friend and classmate Charles Sherrod. Many of you only know his name as one of the founders of SNCC. While in the Marine Corps and in the Navy, I heard the pastor of the one black Baptist church in Jacksonville, North Carolina, while stationed at Camp Lejeune. I heard Richard C. Keller of Virginia Union and I heard his friend, Lacey Curry, when I was stationed at Great Lakes Naval Station.

In the third decade from the ages of twenty-five to thirty-five, I heard yet another vast spectrum of black preaching as I lived in the Washington metropolitan area and then moved in that same decade to Chicago, Illinois. I heard Houston G. Brooks at Mt. Calvary Baptist Church in Rockville, the man who ordained me, and the father of Dr. Henry Brooks, professor at Colgate Rochester Divinity School and Andover Newton School of Theology.

I heard Dr. D. E. King in Chicago. Have any of you all ever heard D. E. King? D. E. King had an earned doctorate from Northern Baptist Seminary in Chicago. D. E. King, for those of you who have never heard of him, was not a whooper. He was not excited in his preaching. D. E. King had a flatline voice. He never raised his voice above this level right here. The night I was introduced to him I had gone to Fellowship Baptist Church in Chicago, where Clay Evans was the pastor. I used to go to Clay Evans's church or First Church of Deliverance on Sunday nights, especially in the early years of Trinity United Church of Christ's development. Our church was really, really cold and I needed to hear something to get my fire burning. So, I'd go sit in the back pew of Fellowship Baptist Church.

Clay Evans didn't know me from Adam's housecat. I just wanted to hear him moan. Clay Evans's broadcast had thirty minutes of music, and they would start singing "What a Fellowship," and of course you don't forget the sick list and then they'd introduce Pastor Evans and he would preach. And Pastor Evans stood up and said, "I see D. E. King is here. Come on up here, D. E. I'm going to let him preach tonight." And now I wanted to leave.

First of all I don't know D. E. King. Secondly, I came to hear you. But, the way Fellowship Church was run and still is run, you don't get up and walk out after the music is finished. The ushers will fight you. I was stuck. I felt sucked. And D. E. King when he stood up, he didn't have a voice like Allan Boesak or Frank Thomas. He said, "I want to preach tonight from Revelation." I said he's got to be a scholar or a fool. "In Revelation, Jesus said behold I am he that was dead and am alive for evermore and I have the keys to hell and heaven. You know before Jesus came everybody who died went to hell." I said to myself, "He's a fool."

From the second sentence on the man had me. He said, "Now by hell I don't mean that lake of fire that y'all mean when you say hell. I'm talking about sheol—sheol, like a waiting station. Something like Catholic purgatory where souls went to wait until the day of resurrection. Jesus, when he died, he went to hell, but he didn't go to wait; he went to carry on a revival. And while he was down there he started preaching." And D. E. King had a vest with a chain across it with about twenty-five keys on the end of the chain. And he pulled out this key chain and said, "He took the first key and he opened up the grave of Abraham. Abraham stood up wiping the cobwebs from his eyes and said—'*Who are you?*' He said—'*I'm that city you were looking for.*' He took the second key and opened up the grave of Isaac, and Isaac said, '*Daddy, who is this?*' He said, '*Don't you remember that wrestling match up on the mountain; the ram in the bushes? He's the one that put the ram there.*' He took the third key and opened up Jacob and Jacob said, '*Granddaddy, who is this?*' '*You remember being down by the River Jabbok, that's who you were wrestling with.*'"

[King] walked through the Old Testament and said, "He took three keys and opened up the graves of Shadrach, Meshach, and Abednego. '*Who is that?*' '*Remember the fourth one in the furnace burning?*'" By the time he got to that last key, he was leading all these folks to heaven and folks at Fellowship were making so much noise, he had a PA system and you couldn't hear him—D. E. King, a masterful homiletician.

I got to hear D. E. King and subsequently had him at our church several times and of course I got to hear Clay Evans. I got to hear Milton Brunson. I got to hear Harold Carter (*Myths That Mire the Ministry* and *The Prayer Tradition of Black People*). I got to hear Henry H. Mitchell. I got to hear Ella Mitchell. I heard Anthony Cardova Campbell. He taught preaching at Boston University and Tony Campbell coined classic phrases for preachers like this: *Sometimes you'll find yourself preaching a sermon so bad you wish it would hurry up and end.*

I heard Walter Fluker. I heard Hycel Taylor. I heard Bishop John Richard Bryant. Prathia Hall Wynn, Brenda Piper Little, Carolyn Knight, Jacqueline Grant, Cecelia Williams Bryant, Bishop H. H. Brookins, Bishop McKinley Young, Yvonne Delk, Fredrick G. Sampson, James Allen Forbes, T. Garrott Benjamin, Cynthia Hale, John W. Kinney, Miles Jerome Jones, and Allan Boesak. I heard black preaching and black preachers from the United States to the Union of South Africa and from the United Holy Church of America to the United Church of Christ.

AFTERWORD

In the fourth decade of my life in ministry from thirty-six to forty-six, I experienced the polarization around social issues at a much more intense level. From the division over the fight to end Apartheid, black preachers who preached divestment like Charles Cobb, Ed Edmonds, and Ben Chavis. And, black preachers who preached constructive engagement like my father's colleague, Leon Sullivan. Black preachers who were open and affirming, like Bishop Yvette Flunder. Black preachers who were radically, if not rabidly, against any notion of inclusivity without conversion from homosexuality to heterosexuality and heterosexism, like Bishop Charles Blake.

And, in that fourth decade, I heard T. L. Barrett one Good Friday at our church. T. L. Barrett was born and raised in the Church of God in Christ, became pastor of a Baptist church and changed it to the Church of Universal Awareness, and is back now to COGIC. But, T. L. Barrett with no seminary education whatsoever came to our church and gave us a seminary education one Good Friday on the word that we assigned him to preach: *Verily verily I say unto you, this day thou shall be with me in Paradise*. And with no seminary education T. L. Barrett said, "Let me help somebody here who's been wondering how Jesus could say to a thief or to a malefactor: *This day you're going to be with me in Paradise*, and then Sunday morning he's raised and Mary sees him; Martha sees him; Peter sees him; Andrew sees him; the Twelve see him; then five hundred more see him." He then said, "It's not a contradiction. Ask these seminary graduates here and they will tell you. In the Greek there is no punctuation. There are no commas, periods, and quotes. And, we are used to seeing the English translation, which says *verily verily I say unto you*—comma, quotation marks—*today you will be with me in Paradise*—period, closed quote." He said, "That's not in the Greek. Look at the Greek. Ain't no commas, quotes. So look at it carefully and you will see Jesus is saying: *Verily verily I say unto you today you are going to be with me in Paradise*—whensoever I get there. I'm saying that to you *today*. Not today you're going to be with me, but whenever I get there you're going to be there."

As I mentioned, Clarence Cobb of Metropolitan Spiritual Church of America, Logan Kearse, his son in the ministry; Henry Harding and Lacy

Banks. Lacy Banks was one of those preachers that those of you who spent all this time in seminary can grow to hate very quickly. Lacy Banks hadn't been anywhere near a seminary, but he was a journalist and he had a facility with words that the wordsmiths today would just kill for. Lacy Banks would put together imageries in his messages that were just awesome like he did while preaching the utterance from the seven last words: "It is finished." Lacy said, "*Jesus took a checklist to heaven and started checking off the stuff that he had done in his ministry. Healed the sick? That's finished! Raised the dead? That's finished!*" Lacy Banks was a sports editor for one of the Chicago newspapers—but he was a powerful preacher.

I heard Jerry Cannon, Katie Cannon—his sister; Robin N. Burkins, Thomas Hoyt. I heard Walter Scott Thomas, William Augustus Jones. I heard Vashti McKenzie, Suzan Johnson Cook, Claudette Copeland, Johnnie Colemon, Michael Eric Dyson, Ann Lightner-Fuller, Frederick Douglas Haynes, Rudolph McKissick, William Curtis, Earl Mason, Marcus Cosby, Lance Watson, and Frank Anthony Thomas.

Now, those of you who know him as a professor and know him as one of the greatest preachers in the country did not know him when he was a seminarian and we had a sleep-in at his house. He kept us up all night when we were trying to get some sleep on a sofa. Here comes Frank. You know one day I'm going to preach a sermon on the woman at the well. Five minutes later. One day I'm going to preach a sermon on the Syro-Phoenician woman. Frank, we're trying to get some sleep. I heard and watched develop one of the most powerful voices in North America—Frank Anthony Thomas.

I heard Teresa Fry Brown, Debra Grant, Jackie Grant's sister, Wilma Johnson, and Vincent Harding. His family asked me to come and preside at his funeral services last year—a high honor. I heard Patricia Gould-Champ, Arlene Churn, Renita Weems, Charles Booth, and Gina Stewart. My exposure to and experience of black preaching and black preachers of ever-widening theological stripes—seminary trained and no seminary training—was giving me an education about assimilation, indoctrination, and orientation that was invaluable; inscrutable at times but invaluable nevertheless.

AFTERWORD

In the fifth decade of my experience straddling the academy and the sanctuary, straddling the academic podium and the free-church pulpit, I saw a split between the Steve Biko supporters and the new Bentley drivers. Black clergy concerned about the poor and black preachers desiring to be somebody's bishop. I saw that rift widen and almost along the same fault lines as Eugene Robinson describes in his book *The Disintegration of Black America*, where the black America that we think we know has disintegrated and is now splintered into four different black Americas. They are (1) the super-rich who don't go to church and don't care nothing about church and don't want to be in church when they go to church, (2) the wannabes who try to pretend like they're the super-rich, (3) the hopelessly poor, and (4) the Africans who are expatriates. They have been here fifteen to twenty-five years and who are part of the black community, who are raising the question and asking our black churches, "How come my kids aren't available for scholarships?" When I went to Lincoln University to speak at a graduation several years ago, both the valedictorian and the salutatorian were Nigerian women who self-defined and considered themselves to be African expatriates living in America.

Almost along the same fault lines that Robinson argues, I have seen the impact that the media and the TV ministries on television have as they splinter the black church into more than four different black churches: praise and worship, social justice, open and affirming, openly homophobic, prosperity only, fixation on soul saving, fixation on mega-sizing and multiple locations, and metropolitan or metroplex ranches. That's what Joe Samuel Ratliff calls them. We no longer have the image of the pastor as a shepherd, but pastors now are ranchers. The pastor sends out Hoss and Little John to take care of the ranch. Many days it feels like we're in the "Mark 5" season of the black church. Our name is legion because there are so many of us. And the demonic metaphor hits painfully close to home in far too many instances.

The demon in Mark 5 says his name is legion. He has hundreds of different personalities. That's what the black church and black preaching feels like for me when I consider the vastly disparate styles of black churches and black preaching in the twenty-first century. Some of what I hear even sounds demonic as idolatry and self-aggrandizement has replaced fidelity to the God of liberation.

And in that fifth decade, forty-seven to fifty-seven, I heard a disturbing variety of black preaching, much of which is eons removed from the Virginia Union University prisms, through which I learned and through which I've viewed substantive black preaching, which was and is faithful to the gospel of Jesus Christ. Consider the complexity during my fifth and sixth decades. I heard Charles Walker of the 19th Street Baptist Philadelphia Church, Frank Madison Reed, Bishop Louis H. Ford, Joe Samuel Ratliff, Otis Moss Jr., and Otis Moss III. I heard James Perkins, Johnny Ray Youngblood, Bishop Nathaniel Jarrett, Bishop Dennis Robinson, and Jessica Ingram.

In the sixth decade, fifty-eight to sixty-eight, and in the seventh decade—on the other hand there's good news. When I hear the preaching of Dionne Boissière, Leslie Callahan, Willie Francois, Jerry Carter, and many of the Millennials, I have hope—and that is good news. And when I hear the wisdom of my oldest grandson. Now that's also good news for me.

My grandson is now in his last semester and will graduate from Yale Divinity School with two degrees in May. But when he was a senior in high school, he was in my car and I was taking him to the youth revival—the last night of the youth revival. He says to me, "Granddaddy, how come Reverend—called the man's name—does not have any social content in his preaching whatsoever?" I said, "I don't know." He said, "You never asked him?" I said, "No." He said, "I'll ask him." Now he's a seventeen-year-old kid in high school. He said, "I'm going to ask him." I said, "Go right ahead!" That night, on the way home, he didn't say anything to me. I waited a week and he still didn't say anything to me. So, I said, "Did you ask Reverend what you said you were going to ask him." "*Yep!*" I said, "What did he say?" He said, "He told me that's not his gift." I said, "How do you respond to that?" He was seventeen years old. He said, "Granddaddy, Uncle Freddy (Frederick Douglas Haynes III) has a gift. He can write out his whole sermon long hand, put it on his PDA, get up in the pulpit, look at it, review it, put his PDA away, and say it word for word, just like actors every week have to learn new lines for television—that's a gift to have that kind of memory. Uncle Rudy—he was talking about Rudolph McKissick—Rudy was a music major in college—voice and organ. He knows exactly what key he's going to whoop in. And when he gets to the end of his sermons, he holds up four fingers to let the musician on the organ know that he is going to start his whoop in A flat and work his way up to the key of C. He's got perfect pitch." My grandson said, "Now *that's* a gift. But to me social content in the message is not a gift; it's a given. How do you follow in the footsteps of him who says: *Behold the Spirit of the Lord God is upon me. He has anointed me to preach the gospel to the poor*; and then to talk about that's not your gift!" Young persons like that who have that kind of consciousness and understanding of what preaching the gospel is, is a sign of hope for me. In fact, I find it priceless!

On the other hand there is the challenging news that Raphael Warnock writes about his observations in *The Divided Mind of the Black Church*, that we quote Jim Cone, but we channel Billy Graham. And, the equally challenging news on the other hand is the megachurch preaching, which is neither pastoral nor prophetic, that is popular with a fixation on two and three locations. Kenyatta Gilbert is very helpful in his work *The Journey and Promise of Black Preaching*, in terms of the threefold nature of the pastoral office, which is prophetic, priestly, and sagely—elderly wisdom, that is, priestly preaching as well as prophetic preaching.

We have the challenge of an assimilated theology where we have forgotten or lost Dr. King's critique of "Americanity" being conflated with Christianity. In King's April 4, 1967, sermon preached at the Riverside Church in New York, King not only critiqued the US involvement in the immoral war in Viet Nam. King named the three-headed demon we are yet facing and fighting—racism, militarism, and capitalism. In assimilated theology, we have moved from Gordon Blaine Hancock's critique of capitalism in the 1930s with the double-duty dollar to an unashamed embrace of capitalism, with women preachers moving from concerns about dedication and integrity to being concerned about being divas and celebrities. Where we have moved from male preachers being more concerned about jewelry than justice. Where we have moved from a position where we were fighting for the freedom of South Africa to a position where they are fascinated with self-aggrandizement.

Prosperity preaching ignores (or blames) the poor. Dr. R. Drew Smith many years ago in 1998 did a two-volume work, *New Day Begun* and *Long March Ahead*, interviewed twenty different church persons—ten chapters in each book—women and men of the gospel in all kinds of occupations preaching, teaching, counseling, asking primarily the essential question, "Where is the black church thirty years after James Cones's *Black Theology and Black Power?* Where is the black church thirty years—1968 to 1998—after King's assassination?" And overwhelmingly the answer was the black church in the days of Martin Luther King confronted an evil government and thirty years later the black church cooperates with an evil government.

But the challenging news in the area of black preaching cannot put out the flame of hope that I see burning in the hearts of this present age of seminarians who have a passion for justice, for mercy, and who are determined to walk where God is walking. I thank Allan Boesak for that insight in his book *The Tenderness of Conscience*, to do justice, to love mercy, and to walk humbly with your God.[3] Ask the people at your church. They'll say that "walking humbly with God" means not to think more highly of yourself than you ought to. Always take the low road. Be humble. No, Boesak explains, it means to walk humbly where God is walking today. To me that translation (and hermeneutic) brings an entirely new meaning to an old song that I love; and I invite you to join me in singing it." *Where he leads me, I will follow.* I will walk humbly with God wherever God is walking and wherever God leads.

And finally, let us pray:

Eternal God, take these who prepare themselves for preaching in your church. Make them and mold them as you would have them after your will. That they may walk with you in the uncomfortable places that you walk today. Through Jesus Christ our Lord we pray.

And all the people of God together will say ... Amen.

---

3. Allan A. Boesak, *The Tenderness of Conscience: African Renaissance and the Spirituality of Politics* (Glasgow, Scotland: Wild Goose Publications, 2008).

Selected Bibliography of African American Preaching

(Disclaimer: The moment you develop a bibliography it is out of date because so many books come out with great regularity.)

Alcantara, Jared E. *Crossover Preaching: Inter-Cultural-Improvisational Homiletics in Conversation with Gardner C. Taylor.* Downer's Grove, IL: InterVarsity Press, 2015.

Allen, Donna E. *Toward a Womanist Homiletic: Katie Cannon, Alice Walker, and Emancipatory Proclamation.* New York: Peter Lang, 2014.

Andrews, Dale P. *Practical Theology for Black Churches: Bridging Black Theology and African American Folk Religion.* Louisville, KY: Westminster John Knox, 2002.

Bailey, E. K. and Warren W. Wiersbe. *Preaching in Black & White: What We Can Learn from Each Other.* Grand Rapids: Zondervan, 2003.

Bond, Adam L. *The Imposing Preacher: Samuel DeWitt Proctor and Black Public Faith.* Minneapolis: Fortress Press, 2013.

Bond, L. Susan. *Contemporary African American Preaching: Diversity in Theory and Style.* St. Louis: Chalice Press, 2003.

Cannon, Katie Geneva. *Teaching Preaching: Isaac Rufus Clark and Black Sacred Rhetoric.* New York: Continuum International Publishing Group, 2002.

Collier-Thomas, Bettye. *Daughters of Thunder: Black Women Preachers and Their Sermons, 1850–1979.* San Francisco: Jossey-Bass, 1997.

Crawford, Evans E., and Thomas H. Troeger. *The Hum: Call and Response in African American Preaching.* Nashville: Abingdon, 1995.

Davis, Gerald L. *I Got the Word in Me and I Can Sing It, You Know: A Study of the Performed African-American Sermon.* Philadelphia: University of Pennsylvania Press, 1985.

Forbes, James A. *The Holy Spirit and Preaching.* Nashville: Abingdon, 1989.

Fry Brown, Teresa L. *Delivering the Sermon: Voice, Body, and Animation in Proclamation.* Minneapolis: Fortress Press, 2008.

———. *Weary Throats and New Songs: Black Women Proclaiming God's Word.* Nashville: Abingdon, 2003.

Gilbert, Kenyatta R. *The Journey and Promise of African American Preaching.* Philadelphia: Fortress Press, 2011.

———. *A Pursued Justice—Black Preaching from the Great Migration to the Civil Rights Movement.* Waco, TX: Baylor Press, 2016.

Harris, James Henry. *Preaching Liberation.* Minneapolis: Fortress Press, 1995.

———. *The Word Made Plain: The Power and Promise of Preaching.* Minneapolis: Fortress Press, 1995.

Haywood, Chanta M. *Prophesying Daughters: Black Women Preachers and the Word, 1823–1913.* Columbia, MO: University of Missouri Press, 2003.

Howard, Gregory. *Black Sacred Rhetoric.* Dallas: Borderstone Press, LLC, 2010.

Johnson, James Weldon, Aaron Douglas, and C. B. Falls. *God's Trombones: Seven Negro Sermons in Verse.* Chapel Hill, NC: University of North Carolina at Chapel Hill Libraries, 2004.

Jones, Kirk Byron. *The Jazz of Preaching: How to Preach with Freedom and Joy.* Nashville: Abingdon, 2004.

LaRue, Cleophus J. *The Heart of Black Preaching.* Louisville, KY: Westminster John Knox, 2000.

———. *I Believe I'll Testify: The Art of African American Preaching.* Louisville, KY: Westminster John Knox, 2011.

———, ed. *More Power in the Pulpit: How America's Most Effective Black Preachers Prepare Their Sermons.* Louisville, KY: Westminster John Knox, 2009.

———, ed. *Power in the Pulpit: How America's Most Effective Black Preachers Prepare Their Sermons.* Louisville, KY: Westminster John Knox, 2002.

———, ed. *This Is My Story: Testimonies and Sermons of Black Women in Ministry.* Louisville, KY: Westminster John Knox, 2005.

Lassiter, Valentino. *Martin Luther King in the African American Preaching Tradition.* Cleveland, OH: Pilgrim Press, 2001.

Lischer, Richard. *The Preacher King: Martin Luther King, Jr. and the Word That Moved America.* New York: Oxford University Press, 1995.

Martin, Lerone A. *Preaching on Wax: The Phonography and the Shaping of Modern African American Religion.* New York: New York University Press, 2014.

Massey, James Earl. *Designing the Sermon: Order and Movement in Preaching.* Abingdon Preacher's Library. Nashville: Abingdon, 1980.

———. *The Responsible Pulpit.* Anderson, IN: Warren Press, 1974.

McMickle, Marvin Andrew. *Preaching to the Black Middle Class: Words of Challenge, Words of Hope.* Valley Forge, PA: Judson Press, 2000.

———. *Shaping the Claim: Moving from Texts to Sermon.* Elements of Preaching. Minneapolis: Fortress Press, 2008.

McClain, William B. *Come Sunday: The Liturgy of Zion.* Nashville: Abingdon, 1990.

Miller, Keith D. *Voice of Deliverance: The Language of Martin Luther King Jr. and Its Sources.* New York: Free Press, 1992.

Mitchell, Ella Pearson. *Those Preaching Women.* 3 vols. Valley Forge, PA: Judson Press, 1985.

Mitchell, Henry H. *Black Preaching: The Recovery of a Powerful Art.* Nashville: Abingdon, 1990.

_____. *Celebration and Experience in Preaching.* Nashville: Abingdon, 1990, rev. 2008.

_____. *The Recovery of Preaching.* San Francisco: Harper & Row Publishers, 1977.

Mitchell, Stephanie Y. *Name It and Claim It: Prosperity Preaching in the Black Church.* Cleveland, OH: Pilgrim Press, 2007.

Moss, Otis III. *Blue Note Preaching in a Post-Soul World: Finding Hope in an Age of Despair.* Louisville, KY: Westminster John Knox, 2015

Moyd, Olin P. *The Sacred Art: Preaching and Theology in the African American Tradition.* Valley Forge, PA: Judson Press, 1995.

Pipes, William H. *Say Amen, Brother! Old-Time Negro Preaching: A Study in American Frustration.* Detroit, MI: Wayne State University Press, 1992.

Powery, Luke. *Spirit Speech: Celebration and Lament in Preaching.* Nashville: Abingdon, 2009.

_____. *Dem Dry Bones: Preaching, Death, and Hope.* Minneapolis: Fortress Press, 2012.

Proctor, Samuel D. *The Certain Sound of the Trumpet: Crafting a Sermon of Authority.* Valley Forge, PA: Judson Press, 1994.

_____. *"How Shall They Hear?" Effective Preaching for Vital Faith.* Valley Forge, PA: Judson Press, 1992.

Roberts, Samuel K., ed. *Born to Preach: Essays in Honor of the Ministry of Henry and Ella Mitchell.* Valley Forge, PA: Judson Press, 2000.

Rosenberg, Bruce A. *Can These Bones Live? The Art of the American Folk Preacher.* Rev. ed. Urbana, IL: University of Illinois Press, 1988.

Salvatore, Nick. *Singing in a Strange Land: C. L. Franklin, the Black Church, and the Transformation of America.* Urbana, IL: University of Illinois Press, 2006.

Simmons, Martha, ed. *Preaching on the Brink: The Future of Homiletics.* Nashville: Abingdon, 1996.

SELECTED BIBLIOGRAPHY OF AFRICAN AMERICAN PREACHING

Simmons, Martha, and Frank A. Thomas. *Preaching with Sacred Fire: An Anthology of African American Preaching, 1750 to the Present.* New York: W. W. Norton & Company, Inc., 2010.

Smith, J. Alfred, *Preach On!* Nashville: Broadman Press, 1984.

Smith, Kelly Miller. *Social Crisis Preaching.* Macon, GA: Mercer University Press, 1984.

Spencer, Jon Michael. *Sacred Symphony: The Chanted Sermon of the Black Preacher.* New York: Greenwood Press, 1987.

Stephens, Alfred. *Homiletics from the Underside: The Art of Contextual Preaching.* Madurai, India: ECHO, 2014.

Stewart, Warren H. *Interpreting God's Word in Black Preaching.* Valley Forge, PA: Judson Press, 1984.

Taylor, Gardner C. *How Shall They Preach?* Elgin, IL: Progressive Baptist Publishing House, 1977.

Thomas, Frank A. *Preaching as Celebration Digital Lecture Series and Workbook.* Indianapolis: Hope for Life Press, 2015.

_____. *They Like to Never Quit Praisin' God: The Role of Celebration in Preaching.* Cleveland, OH: United Church Press, 1997.

Titon, Jeff Todd. *Give Me This Mountain: Life, History, and Selected Sermons of C. L. Franklin.* Urbana, IL: University of Illinois Press, 1989.

Travis, Sarah. *Decolonizing Preaching: The Pulpit as Postcolonial Space.* Eugene, OR: Cascade Books, 2014.

Turner, William Clair Jr. *Preaching That Makes the Word Plain: Doing Theology in the Crucible of Life.* Eugene, OR: Cascade Books, 2008.

Warren, Mervyn A. *King Came Preaching: The Pulpit Power of Dr. Martin Luther King, Jr.* Downers Grove, IL: InterVarsity Press, 2001.

Wherry, Peter M. *Preaching Funerals in the Black Church: Bringing Perspective to Pain.* Valley Forge, PA: Judson Press, 2014.

Appendix A
"His Own Clothes"

by Gardner C. Taylor

And when they had mocked him, they took off the purple from him and put his own clothes on him. Then they led him out to crucify him. (Mark 15:20 NIV)

Short of the cross itself and the betrayal by Judas, what the soldiers did to Jesus may well have been the most humiliating part of our Lord's suffering and death for you and me. We may be greatly wronged and deeply hurt, but we want to be able to hold on to our human dignity, the feeling that we are a part of the family of humankind. Great suffering may be visited upon us, but there can be a certain nobility, a mark of grandeur, in the way people hold their heads high and bear bravely whatever it is they must go through.

There is something uniquely cruel in being laughed at and mocked, set apart from one's fellows and made the target of ugly jibes, cruel comment, and cutting laughter. One of the most painful and sinister weapons used historically against black people in this country was mockery and ridicule. Physical features were caricatured and exaggerated, and so the large white-lipped, wide-eyed, blackened faces in minstrel shows became the notion of the way black people looked and acted. I am not far enough from the experience of that mockery to be able to see the art in this kind of thing, no matter what the occasion may be. The purpose of the foot-shuffling, head-scratching, wide-grinning, ghost-frightened darky was to ridicule, scorn, and humiliate. Every southern town once had its village idiot whom children would shamefully taunt. Children who are different know how cruel such horseplay can be.

Far crueler than our own experience was the kind of scorn and ridicule that the soldiers heaped upon our Lord on the night leading to his crucifixion. While it may be true that the sport these members of the praetorian guard, Pilate's military escort, made of Jesus had little venom in it, still it chills the spirit to think of the Son of God, the Savior of the world, the blessed Redeemer, being the object of the rude jokes and the broad barracks' humor of these rough and dull-witted soldiers.

The Master moved toward his death on our behalf over a road that grew constantly more steep and more terrifying. First, there was his inner agony in Gethsemane. This was followed by betrayal, after which the chains were put on Jesus as a common criminal. Later that night they blindfolded our Lord and then struck him a stinging slap in the face taunting, "Prophesy. Who is it that smote thee?" Then they did spit in his face to add to the outrage. Each new assault seemed designed to outdo the last.

Following all of these things, they scourged the Lord. This painful humiliation probably took place on the platform where the trial had been held and in sight of all. The victim was stripped down to the waist and was stretched against a pillar with hands tied. The instrument of torture was a long leather strip, studded with pieces of lead and bits of bone. The whip left lashes, and the lead and bone tore out chunks of flesh. Some died under the lash, and others emerged from the torture raving mad. Through all of these things Jesus passed in the interest of all of our souls. All of these things, as horrible and as appalling as they are, were but preliminary and secondary to the supreme sacrifice of Calvary. So we read that after the Lord was scourged with the lash, sentence was pronounced, and it was the sentence of death by crucifixion, the most awful and painful of the Roman methods of execution. Cicero declared that it was "the most cruel and horrifying death." (William Barclay thought that the Romans picked up this method of execution from the Persians, who believed the earth was sacred and wished to avoid defiling it with an evildoer.) Lifted on a cross, the condemned slowly died, and the vultures and carrion crows might dispose of the body.

The Roman ritual of condemnation and execution was fixed. Sentence was pronounced, "Let him be crucified." The sentence was that this man should be hung on the cross. Then the judge turned to the guard and said, "Go, soldier, and prepare the cross." It was at this point that Jesus our Lord was turned over to the soldiers who formed the personal guard of Pilate as governor. These men were hard-bitten professional soldiers who chafed at their unpleasant assignment in such a hot, fly-ridden place as Palestine and among all of those strange and offensive people. They took their pastime and sport when and where they could find them. One of their pleasures was to taunt and torture convicted criminals who cringed before them like cornered and helpless animals. The Son of God was turned over to them, and they went to work with their cruel jibes.

The whole detachment gathered in their barracks with the Savior of the world before them and, as they thought, in their hands. They stripped him of his clothes. Having picked up some thread of the charge that Jesus claimed to be a king, they jammed a reed in his hand to mock a scepter, plaited a crown made out of thorn bush for his brow, and flung around the Lord's shoulder an old, faded red tunic, the scarlet cloak that was a part of the parade uniform of the Roman soldier. All this was done to mock him as a king, and so they bowed down in ridicule as if to honor and worship him. "We will be your devotees and subjects, King Jesus. Look at us kneeling before you," and then their loud, uncouth laughter rang and echoed through the barracks.

There are still many who put cloaks of imitation honor and false respect on the Lord Jesus as surely as those soldiers put their old scarlet robe on the Savior. Such do not mean their patronizing words of respect about the Lord Jesus. You can hear them now and again. One says, "I respect and honor Jesus. His golden rule is enough religion for anybody to live by. I admire his life and believe it to be a thing of beauty. His ethics are splendid principles of conduct and human relations."

As for his church and all of that, these smart people are very lofty: "It is all right for those who need it, but I do not go to church. I do not feel the need of it, really." And so saying, they feel they have delivered themselves of something very profound and, if not profound, then chic and fashionable. Well, I had a dog, a blooded Doberman pinscher, who never went to church either. I feel like answering such glib dismissal of the church for which Christ died by saying, "My dog did not go to church either. He never felt the need of it because he was a dog. Now, what is your reason?"

APPENDIX A

There are still others who put garments of mock royalty on the Lord and who call his name but who feel no deep loyalty to him, no crowning and controlling love for the Lord, who has done so much for us. You may see them now and again in church, now and then among the people of Christ. They throw their leftovers at the Lord who made us all, as one would toss scraps to a pet dog. They are neither hot nor cold, and to such the word of the Revelation applies, "I will spue thee out of my mouth" (3:16 KJV).

There is a lot of sham religion in this country, people going through the motions for whom Christ is not a living, determining presence. Again and again people ask, "What is wrong with us as a nation?" One word is the answer: godlessness. Never mind the churches and synagogues and mosques; godlessness is what is wrong with us. Never mind the public prayers and taking oaths on the Bible. Godlessness is what is wrong with America. How does it come out? In the swagger of a gun lobby and money that stops congressmen from passing a gun law. In greed and bigotry and the attitude "anything goes." In lies and deceit in a nation that has no room for worship or things of the spirit.

You ask what is wrong with us as a people. Listen to any national telecast. See how all of our national interest is built around what some self-serving people in Washington do: crime, scams, confusion. See how little of the heart and mind, how little room for things of the spirit, there is in our national telecasts. Godlessness! And until we turn to the Lord, it will not get better; it will get worse. And, yes, one thing after another will go wrong.

Have I put fake garments on the Lord Jesus? Have I cloaked the Savior of the world in scarlet robes of pretense, claiming that I honor him as Lord while my heart is far from him? Do I take my faith in the Lord Jesus seriously? Am I willing, as George Eliot put it, to sacrifice anything for him as long as the result is not unpleasant?

And then we read that when the soldiers had tired of their ugly game of ridicule and making sport of the Son of God, they took off the old scarlet tunic and put his own clothes back on him. This was the final preparation for crucifixion. They put on our Lord his own clothes. And "his own clothes" says worlds to us. We need to see him as he is, "in his own clothes," not mocked and ridiculed by false respect and pious hypocrisy. When we see the Lord "in his own clothes," in his true character and force, we see someone who makes us cry out for forgiveness and for his good favor and approval. Looking at Jesus as he is, we see ourselves as we are.

When our Christ is not mocked by false garments of respectable sneer or false enthusiasm, when we see him in his own clothes as he is, we want to do better. Dr. Donald Shelby, the California United Methodist preacher, has told of a terrible storm on Lake Michigan in which a ship was wrecked near the shore. A Northwestern University student, Edmond Spenser, went into the raging water again and again and single-handedly rescued seventeen people. When friends carried him to his room, nearly exhausted and faint, he kept asking them, "Did I do my best?" In the presence of Christ we ask, "Lord, did I do my best?" I am a preacher, and each time I preach I must ask, "Lord, did I do my best?" Officer, choir member, usher, did you do your best?

Jesus in his own clothes going to Calvary did his best. His garments on that lonely hill were rolled in blood, making understandable the old cry of Isaiah, "Who is this that cometh from Edom, with dyed garments from Bozrah? this that is glorious in his apparel, travelling in the greatness of his strength? (Isa 63:1 KJV). We ask, "Wherefore art thou red in thine apparel, and thy garments [thy clothes] like him that treadeth in the winefat?" (v. 2 KJV). And he answers, "I have trodden the winepress alone. . . . For the day of vengeance is in mine heart, and the year of my redeemed is come" (vv. 3-4 KJV).

In his own clothes he went to Calvary and made everything all right, not temporarily all right but for always. At Calvary Christ was at his best. Nothing had been left undone. On no other day does Jesus have to go back to finish his work at Calvary. This he did once. "Now once in the end of the world hath he appeared to put away sin by the sacrifice of himself. . . . So Christ was once offered to bear the sins of many" (Heb 9:26, 28). He died in his own clothes as Savior and Redeemer. Once for all. It is all right now. The crooked way has been made straight; we may arise and shine for light is come. It is all right now.

166 We shall see him yet in other clothes. Ellen White, the prophetess
167 of Seventh-Day Adventism, pictures that day when Christ shall appear
168 no longer with an old, faded red cloak around his shoulders, no longer
169 mocked by soldiers, no longer wearing simple garments of this earth. Ev-
170 ery eye shall see him. We will see him as heaven's King, victor over death,
171 hell, and the grave, the admired of angels. Every eye shall see him. Ten
172 thousand times ten thousand and thousands and thousands of angels and
173 the triumphant sons and daughters of God will escort him. His raiment
174 will outshine the sun. And on his vesture, his clothes, a name will be writ-
175 ten, "King of kings and Lord of lords." Shall we not shout his name who
176 has lifted us to heights sublime and made us his own people forever?

CPSIA information can be obtained
at www.ICGtesting.com
Printed in the USA
LVHW040412180820
663493LV00022B/2216

9 781501 818943